Paris Ontario Book 2 in Colour Photos, Saving Our History One Photo at a Time

Photography
by Barbara Raué
2017

Series Name:
Cruising Ontario

Book 178: Paris Book 2

Cover photo: 42 Broadway Street East, Page 11

Series Name: Cruising Ontario
Saving Our History One Photo at a Time
in colour photos

Books Available in Alphabetical Order:
Aberfoyle, Acton, Alton, Amherstburg, Ancaster, Arthur, Aylmer, Ayr, Bloomingdale, Brantford, Burlington, Caledon, Caledonia, Cambridge, Clifford, Conestogo, Delhi, Dorchester to Aylmer, Drayton, Drumbo, Dryden, Dundas, Eden Mills, Elmira, Elora, Essex, Fergus, Guelph, Hagersville, Hamilton, Hanover, Harriston, Hespeler, Jarvis, Kenora, Kingston, Kingsville, Kitchener, Linwood, Listowel, London, Lucknow, Midland, Mono, Mount Forest, Neustadt, New Hamburg, Niagara-on-the-Lake, Oakville, Orangeville, Orillia, Ottawa, Owen Sound, Palmerston, Penetanguishene, Peterborough, Petrolia, Port Elgin, Preston, Rockwood, Sarnia, Seaforth, Sheffield, Shelburne, Simcoe, Southampton, St. Jacobs, St. Marys, St. Thomas, Stoney Creek, Stratford, Thamesford, Tillsonburg, Waterdown, Waterford, Waterloo, Welland, Wellesley, Windsor, Wingham, Woodstock

Book 157: Brockville
Book 158: Merrickville
Book 159: Smiths Falls
Book 160: Portland, Newboro
Book 161: Westport & Area
Book 162: Perth
Book 163-166: Belleville
Book 167-168: Port Colborne
Book 169: Erin in Colour
Book 170: Goderich in Colour
Book 171: Sault Ste. Marie
Book 172: Lake Superior
Book 173-176: Thunder Bay

Book 177-179: Paris

Other Books by Barbara Raue

Coins of Gold

Arrows, Indians and Love

The Life and Times of Barbara
Volume 1: Inventions That Have Enhanced My Life
Volume 2: Entertainment That I Have Enjoyed
Volume 3: East Coast Trips
Volume 4: Olympics Have Always Intrigued Me
Volume 5: Wonders of the World
Volume 6: Caribbean Cruises We Have Enjoyed
Volume 7: Animals
Volume 8: Storms and Other Major Disasters in My Lifetime
Volume 9: Wars, Terrorist Attacks and Major Disasters

The Cromwell Family Book

Laura Secord Discovered

Daddy Where Are You?

Montana Series
Book 1: Montana Dream
Book 2: Life on the Montana Frontier
Book 3: Montana to Boston and Back
Book 4: Montana Sons Go to War
Book 5: Montana Sons Return From War

Visit Barbara's website to view all of her books
http://barbararaue.ca

Paris

Paris, Ontario is located on the Grand River. It was first settled by Hiram Capron a native of Vermont who, in 1822, emigrated to Norfolk County where he helped to establish one of Upper Canada's earliest iron foundries. He settled here at the Forks of the Grand (where the Grand and Nith Rivers meet) in 1829, divided part of his land into town lots, and in 1830 constructed a grist-mill and named the town after the gypsum deposits that were mined nearby. Gypsum is used to make plaster of Paris.

The use of cobblestones to construct buildings was introduced to the area by Levi Boughton when he erected St. James Church in 1839; this was the first cobblestone structure in Paris. Two churches and ten homes, all in current use, are made of numerous such stones taken from the rivers. Other architectural styles that are visible in the downtown area include Edwardian, Gothic and Post Modern.

Dominion Day 1879 began at six a.m. with the ringing of all the town bells. Sports and games were played throughout the day - lacrosse, cricket, boat races, jumping contests, and foot races with prizes for the winners. In the evening there were bonfires and fireworks.

Since its earliest days, Paris was the site of gypsum beds. When ground to a powder in a mill, gypsum, or Plaster of Paris, could be used as a fertilizer, to coat the interior walls of a home, or for casts to set broken bones.

Jim Percival created scale models of the thirteen cobblestone buildings in Paris.

Table of Contents

Broadway Street East	Page 6
Grand River Street North	Page 12
River Lane	Page 24
William Street	Page 24
Charlotte Street	Page 30
Emily Street	Page 32
West River Street	Page 34
John Avenue	Page 38
Banfield Street	Page 40
Jane Street	Page 56
Architectural Terms	Page 62
Building Styles	Page 66

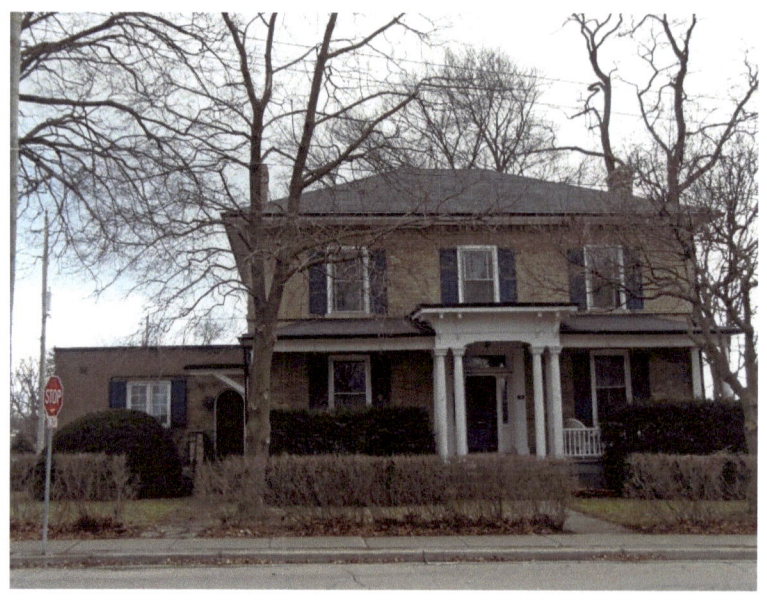

19 Broadway Street East – Italianate, hipped roof, sidelights and transom window

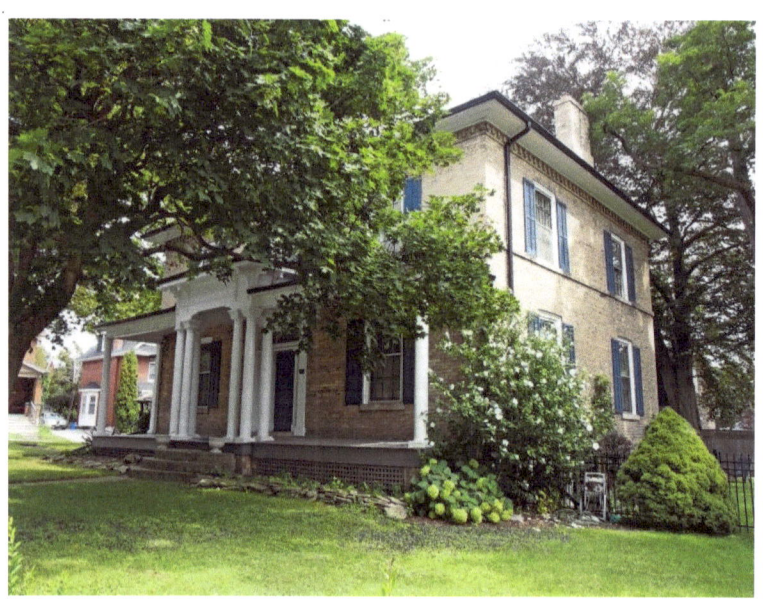

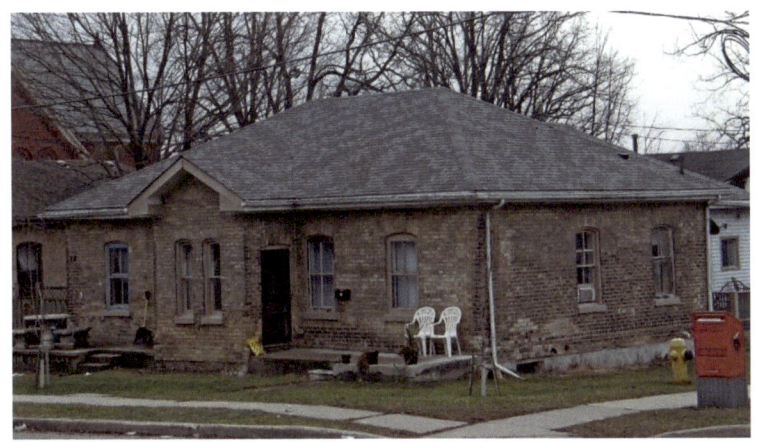

13 Broadway Street East – Regency Cottage

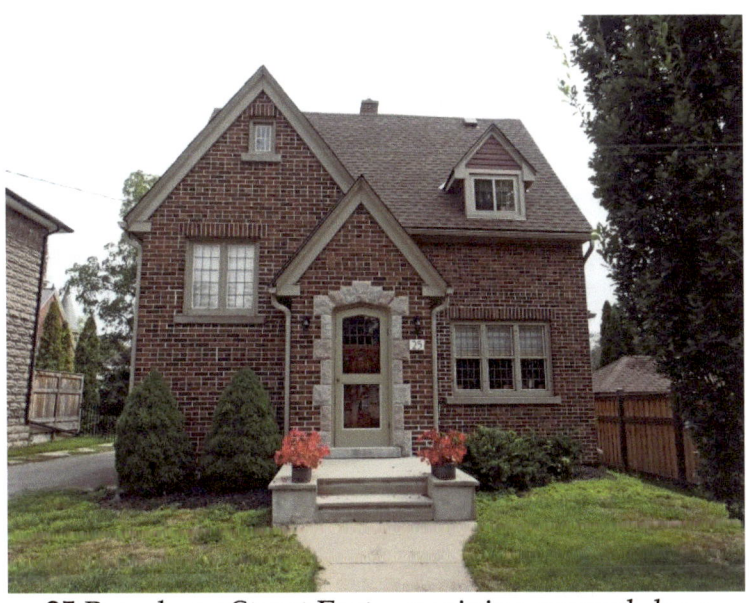

25 Broadway Street East – quoining around door

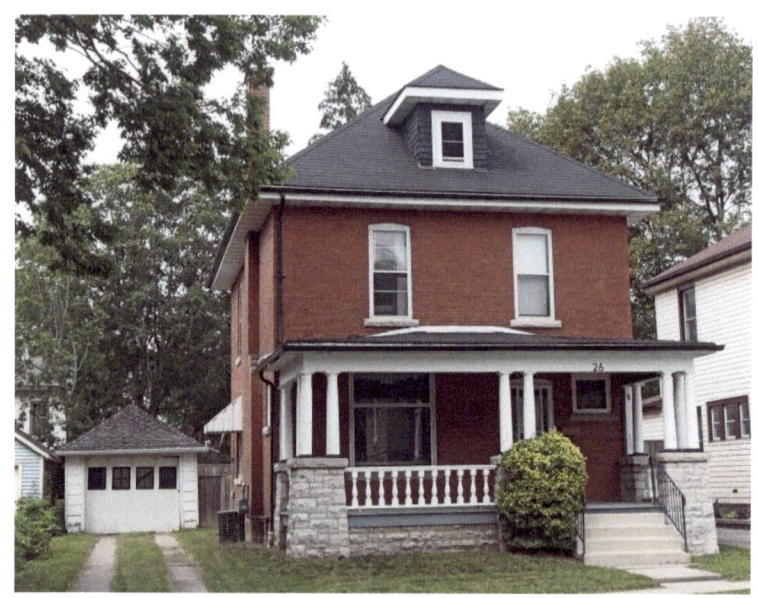

26 Broadway Street East – hipped roof, dormer

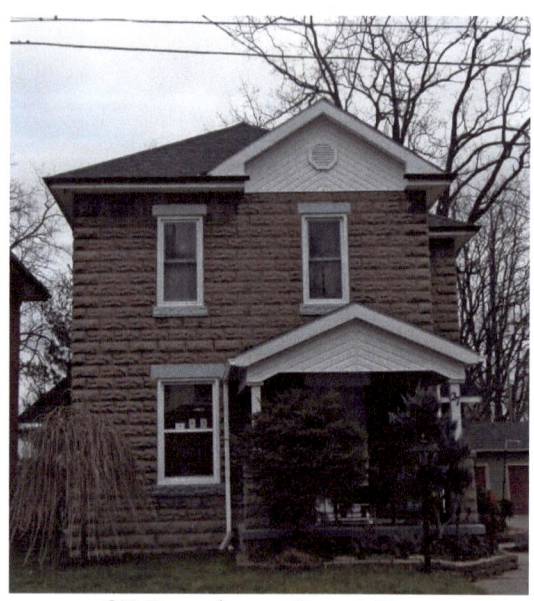

27 Broadway Street East

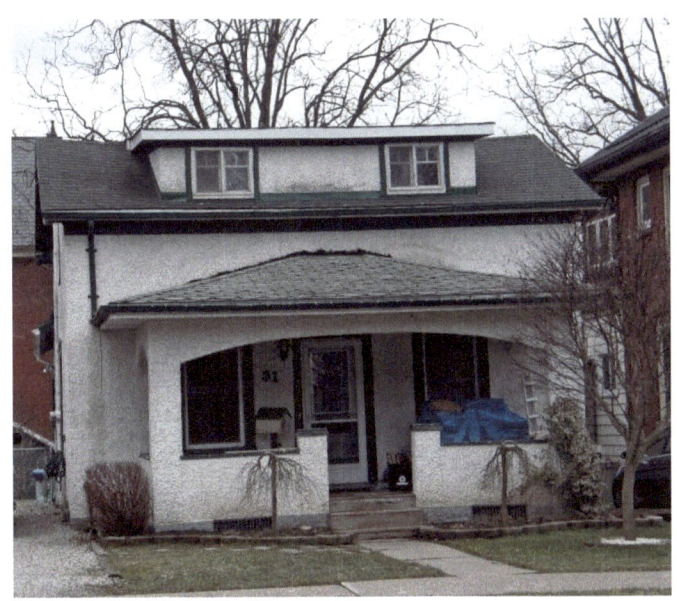

31 Broadway Street East – dormer in attic

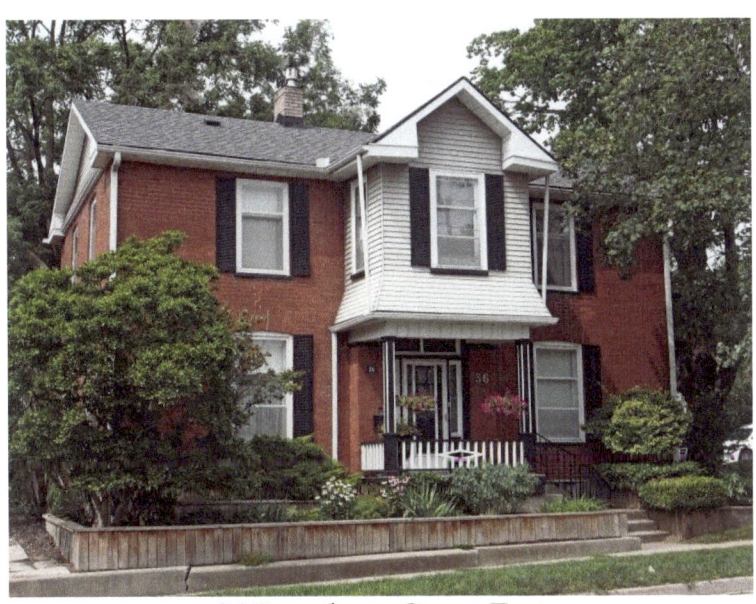

36 Broadway Street East

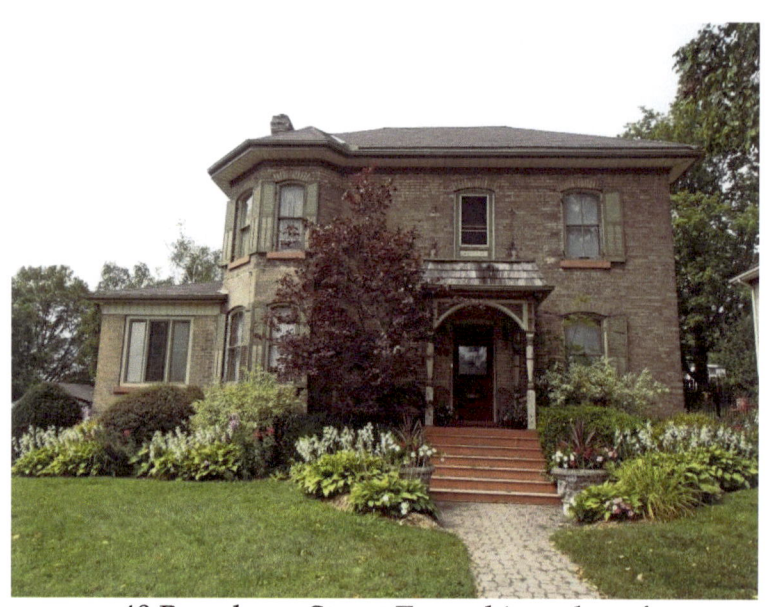

40 Broadway Street East – hipped roof

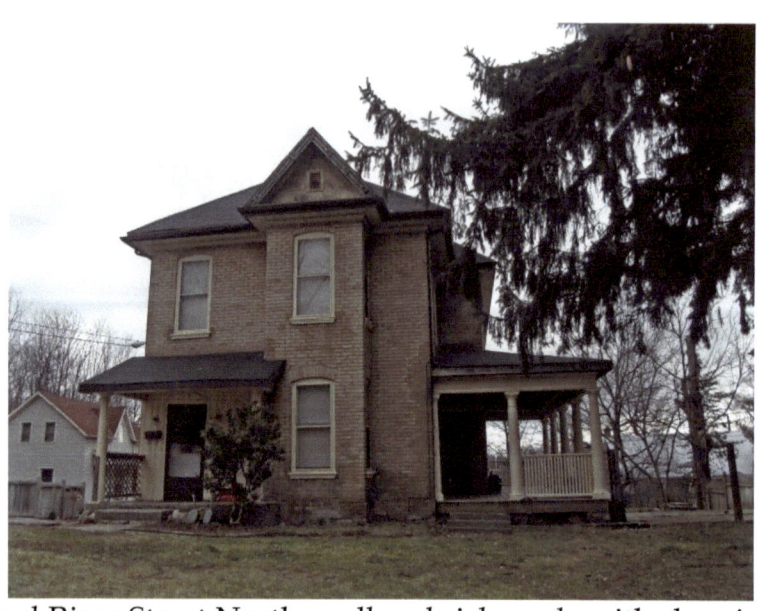

Grand River Street North - yellow brick made with clay rich in lime

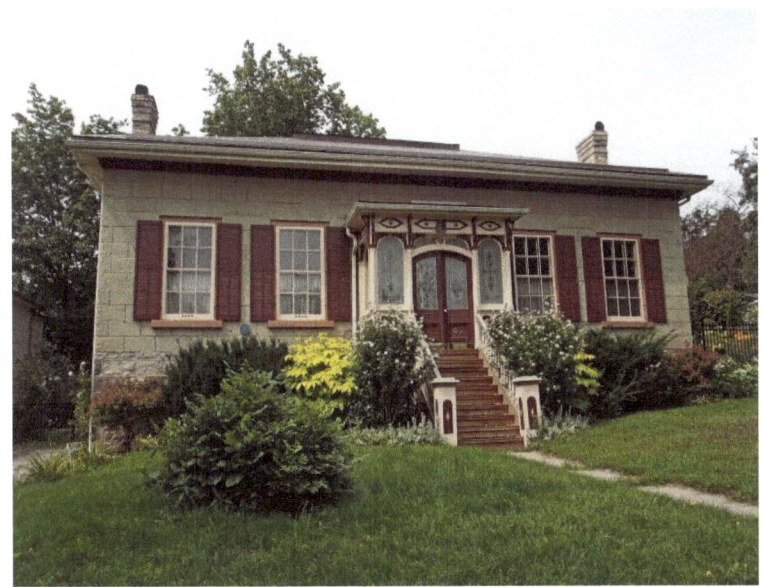

42 Broadway Street East – Gouinlock House - is a one-storey, rubble-stone, building constructed in 1845. The Gouinlock House is associated with John Penman, one of Paris's leading early industrialists and the cofounder of the Penman Manufacturing Company Limited. Penman rented this home, in the mid-1880s, while his permanent residence, Penmarvian, was under renovation. The Gouinlock House is thought to be the only solid rubble-stone building in Paris. This home features local materials and skilled craftsmanship. The exterior of the home was parging and etched to resemble cut stone blocks or coursed ashlar. The more notable features of this home include the large windows, the chimneys, the etched glass doors and the woodwork. Though both the enclosed verandah and a rear portion of the home were additions, the use of rubble-stone and the sympathetic design maintained the integrity of the home.

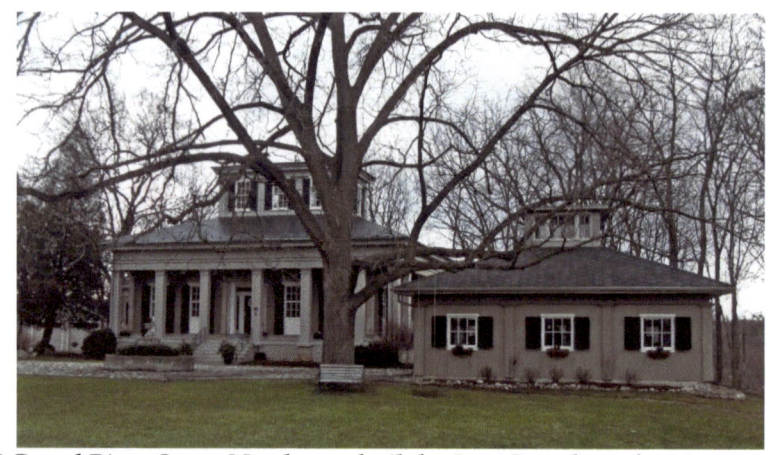

165 Grand River Street North was built by Levi Boughton for Norman and Elizabeth Hamilton, Americans who arrived in Paris about 1831. Norman was a wealthy local industrialist, miller and brewer. This three-storey cobblestone building is designed in the Greek Revival style c. 1839-1844 – it appears to be 1½-storeys in height – the second storey windows are set in light-wells in the verandah roof and are concealed from view by the deep architrave of the verandah. The pillars are square. The triple hung windows on the front façade can be opened so that you can walk out onto the verandah. A lower basement walk-out floor exits to the rear yard. The Hamilton's son-in-law, Paul Wickson, used the belvedere as his art studio; he specialized in painting animals and rural scenes. An addition was added in 1861 to accommodate visiting family members.

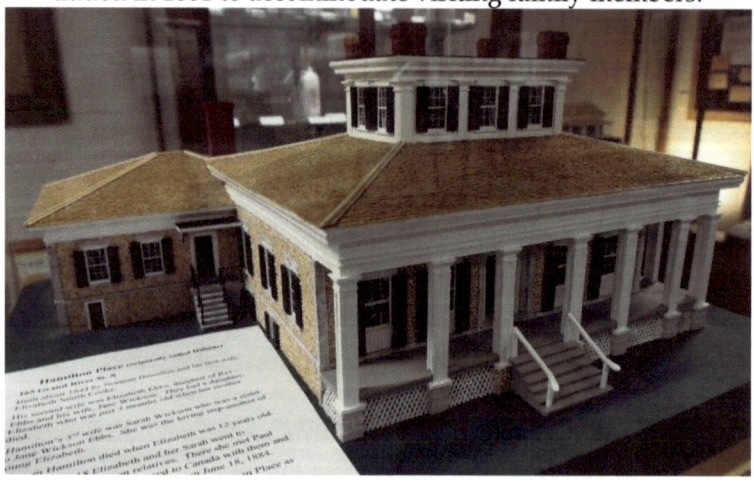

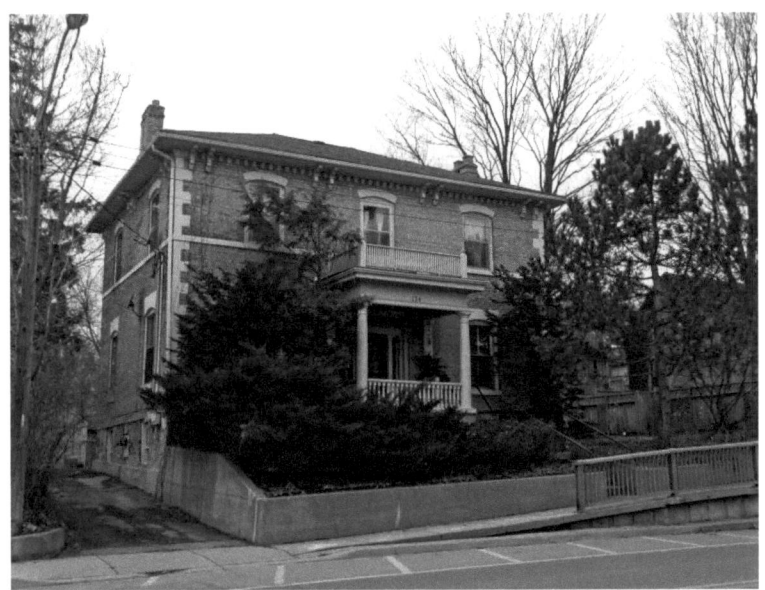

174 Grand River Street North – Italianate – hipped roof, corner quoins, dentil molding

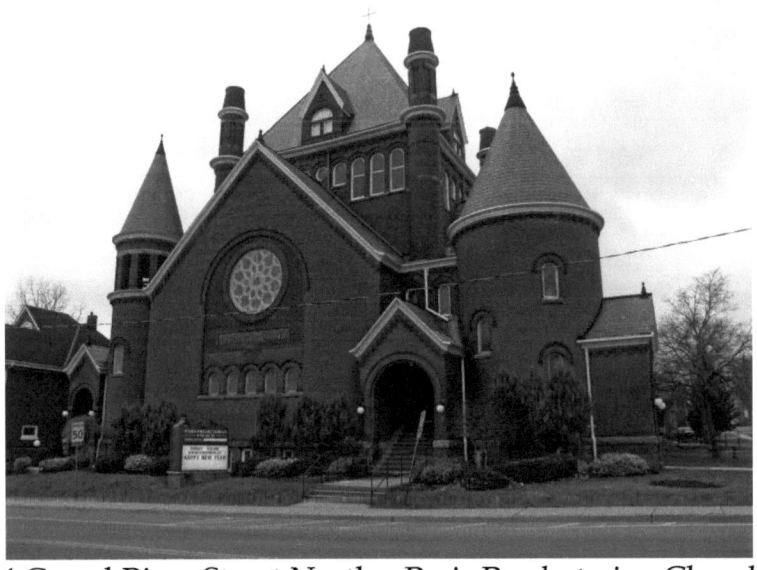

164 Grand River Street North – Paris Presbyterian Church – Romanesque Revival design built in 1893 - turrets, conical towers, round stained glass rose window, terra cotta detailing

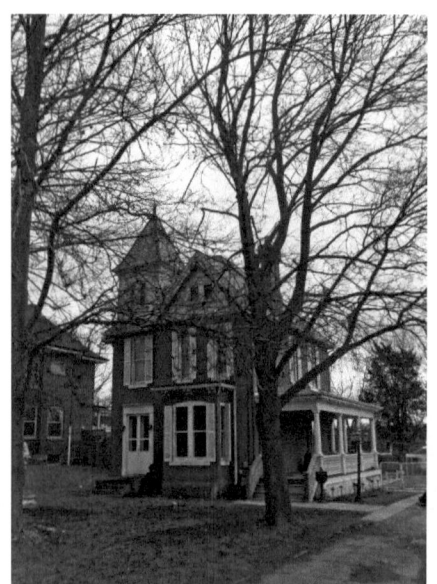 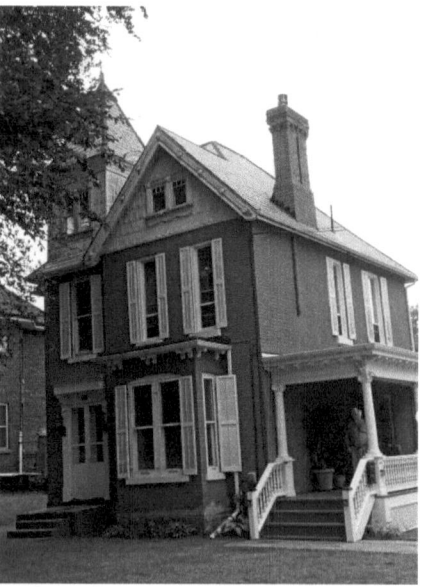

173 Grand River Street North – three-storey tower

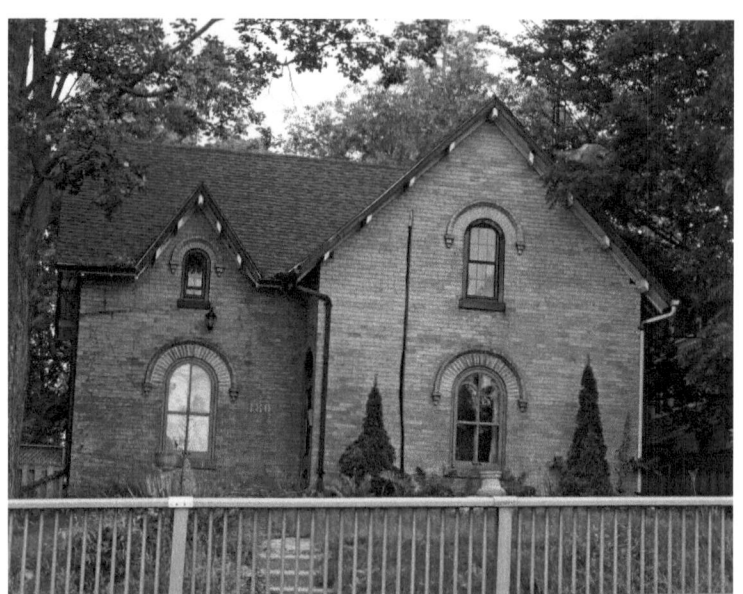

180 Grand River Street North – Gothic - decorative window voussoirs

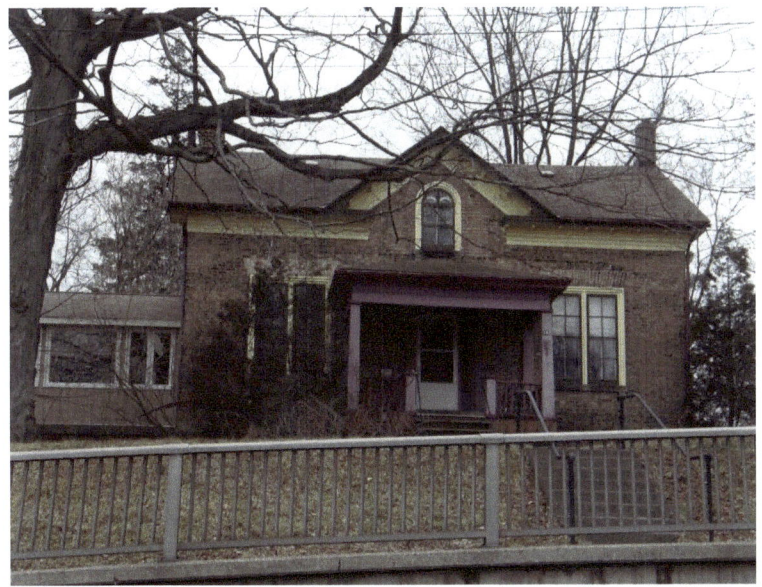

182 Grand River Street North – Gothic cottage – yellow brick

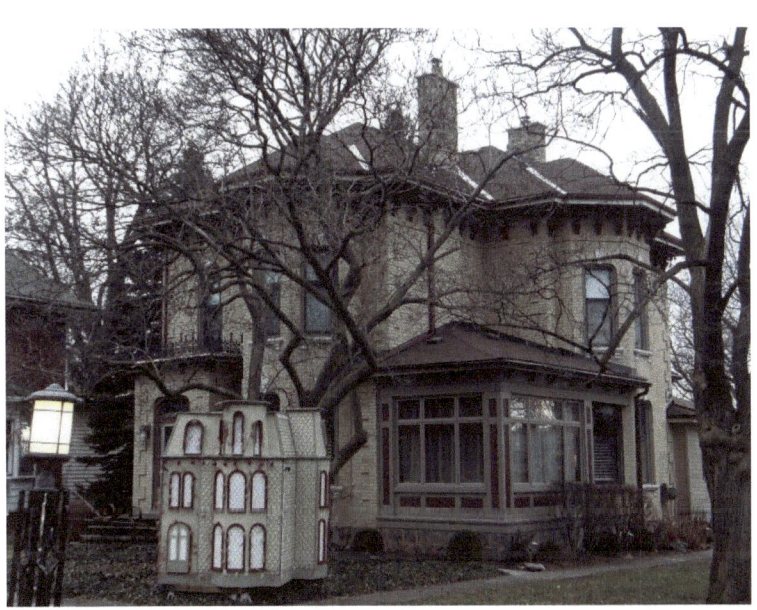

Grand River Street North – Italianate style

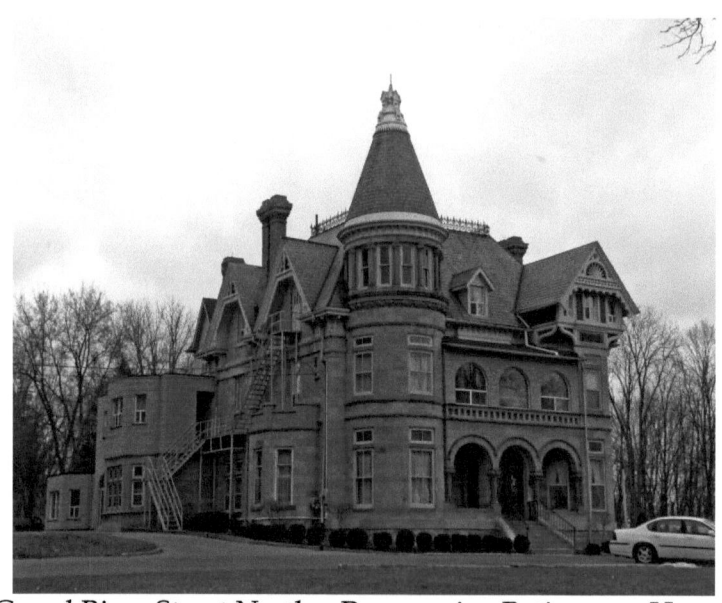

185 Grand River Street North – Penmarvian Retirement Home was built in 1845 by the founder of Paris, Hiram Capron, as a modest two storey building. In 1887 local industrialist John Penman purchased the home and added the Victorian turrets, towers and arches.

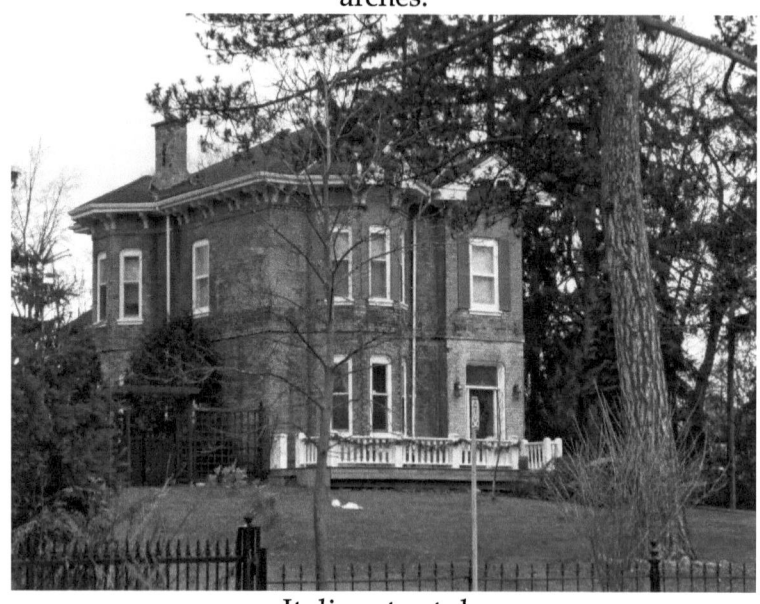

Italianate style

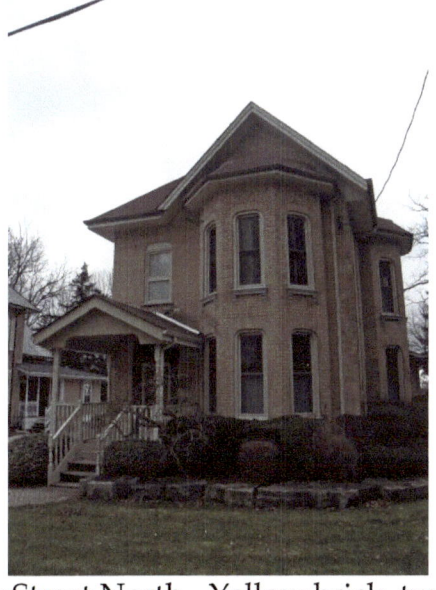

Grand River Street North - Yellow brick, two storey bay window, round windows

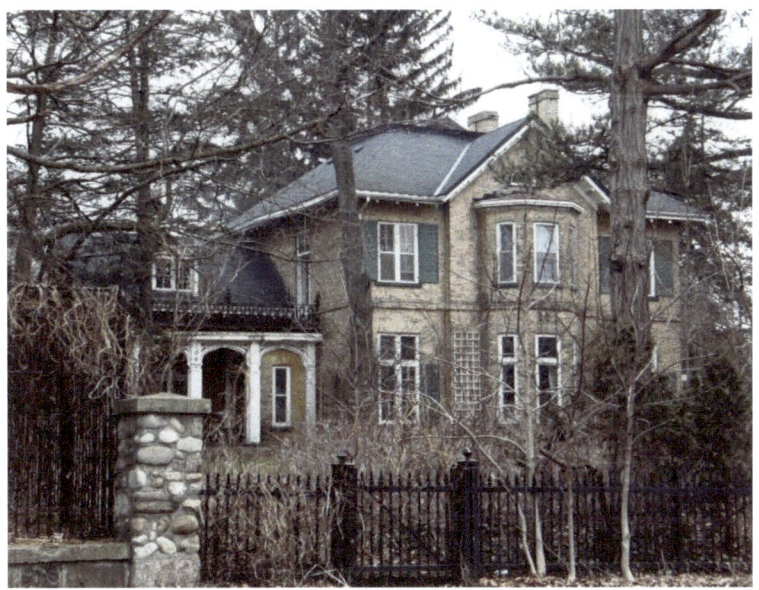

Grand River Street North

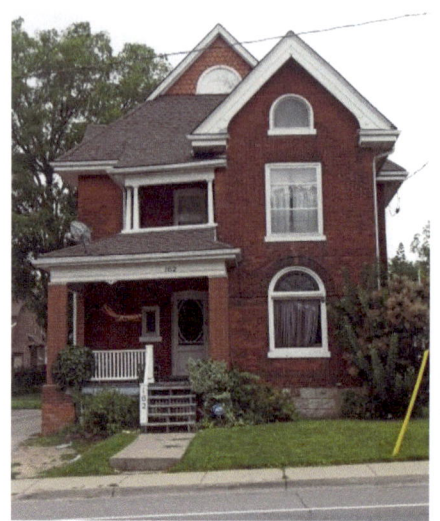

162 Grand River Street North   Grand River Street North

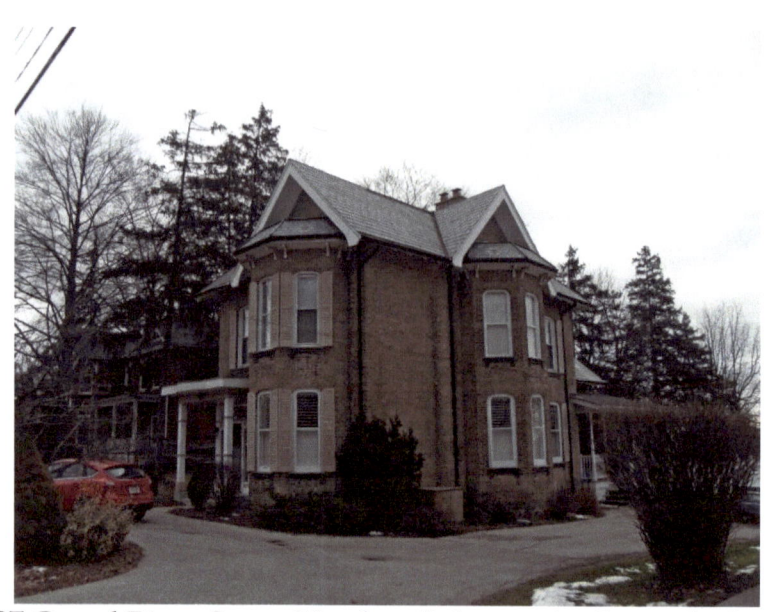

197 Grand River Street North – dichromatic tile work above two-storey bay windows

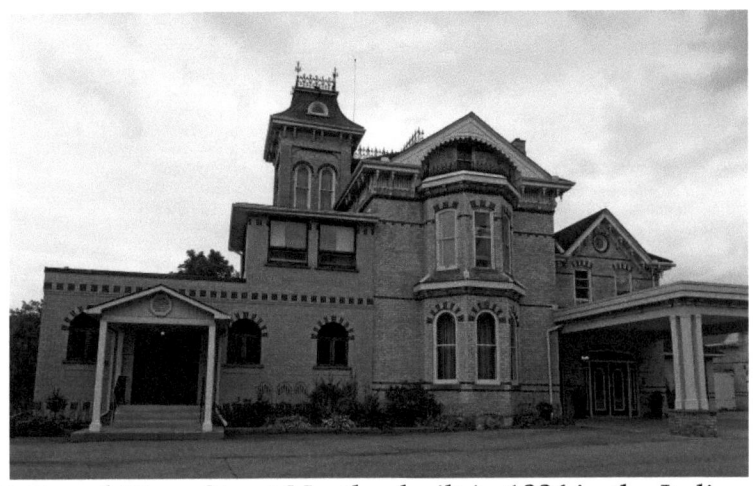

184 Grand River Street North – built in 1886 in the Italianate style for Captain Cox who was Postmaster of Paris – square tower with half-round windows, iron cresting on roof top; dichromatic brickwork – now the William Kipp Funeral Home

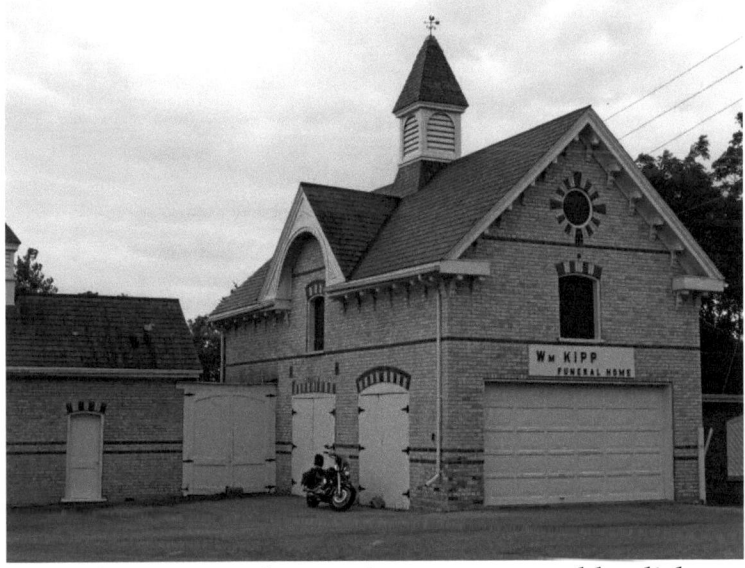

Carriage House – cupola, cornice return on gable, dichromatic brickwork

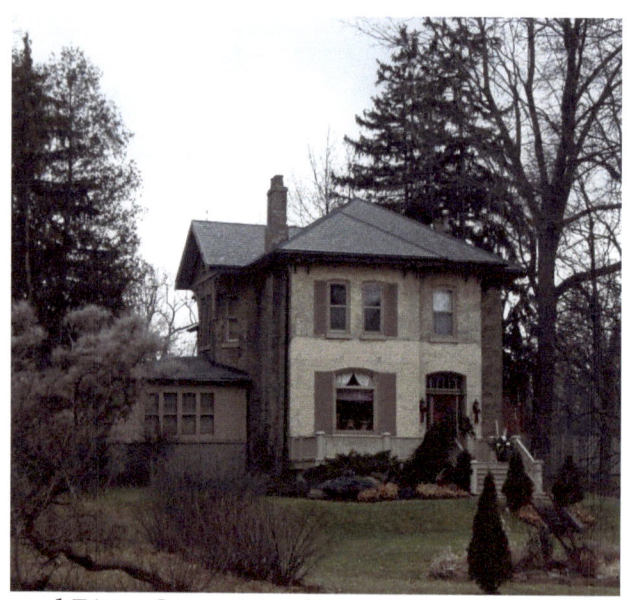

201 Grand River Street North – yellow brick – "Elmhurst" built in 1895

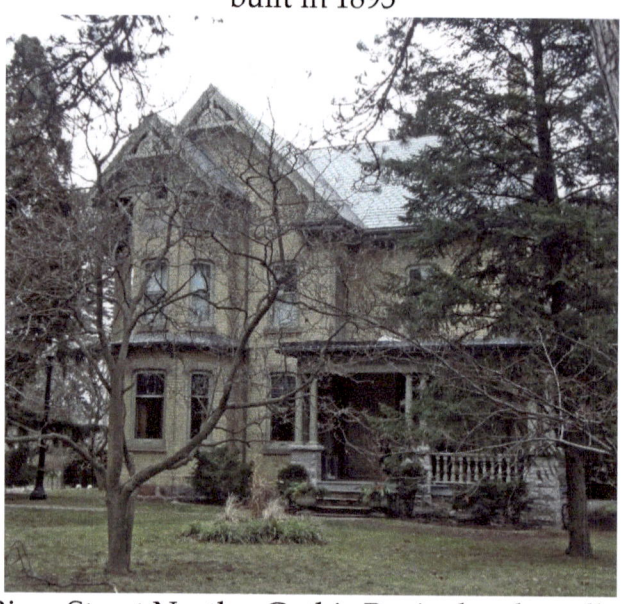

Grand River Street North – Gothic Revival style, yellow brick, two-storey bay window, verge board trim on gables

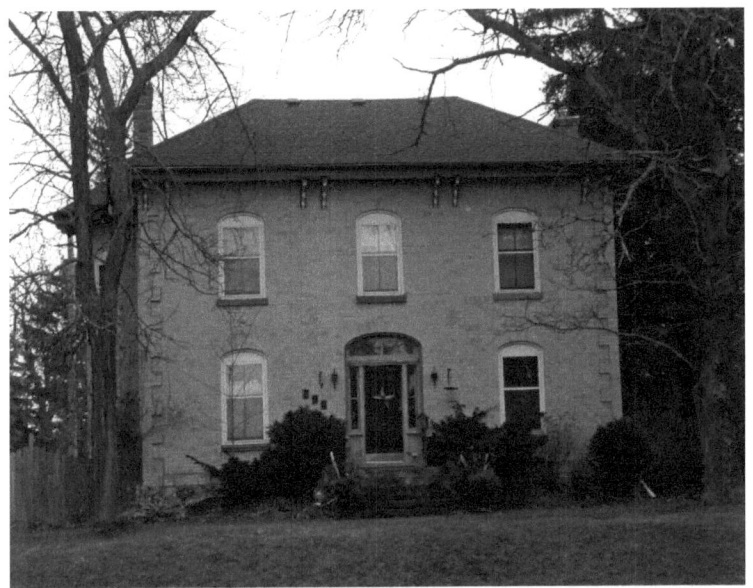

204 Grand River Street North – Italianate style – paired cornice brackets, yellow brick, quoins on corners

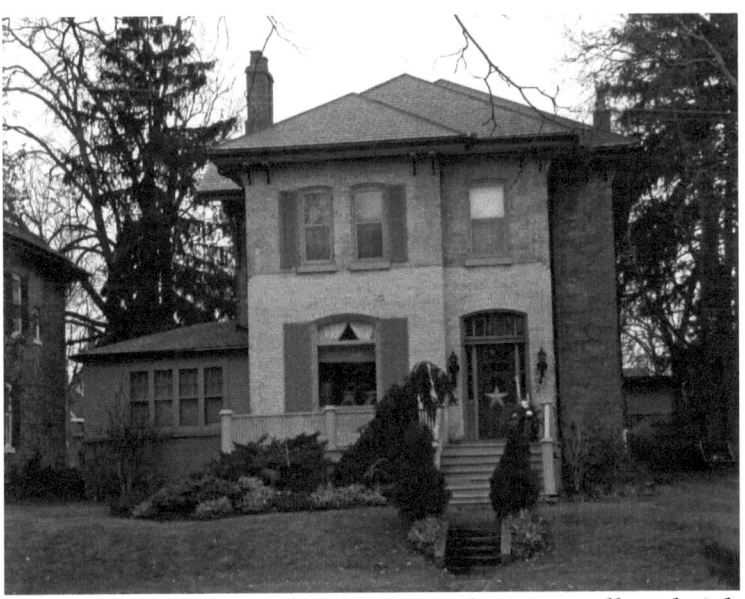

202 Grand River Street North – Italianate, yellow brick

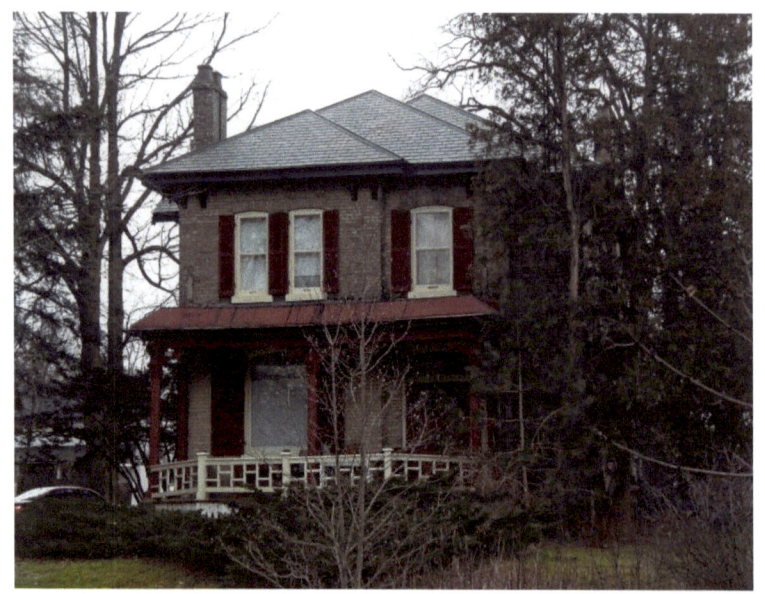

Grand River Street North – yellow brick, triple level roof

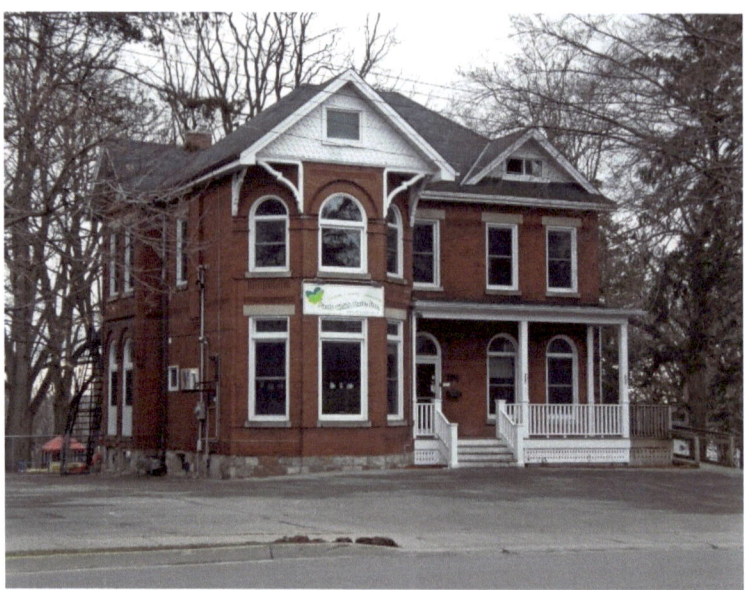

199 Grand River Street North – red brick – Edwardian style

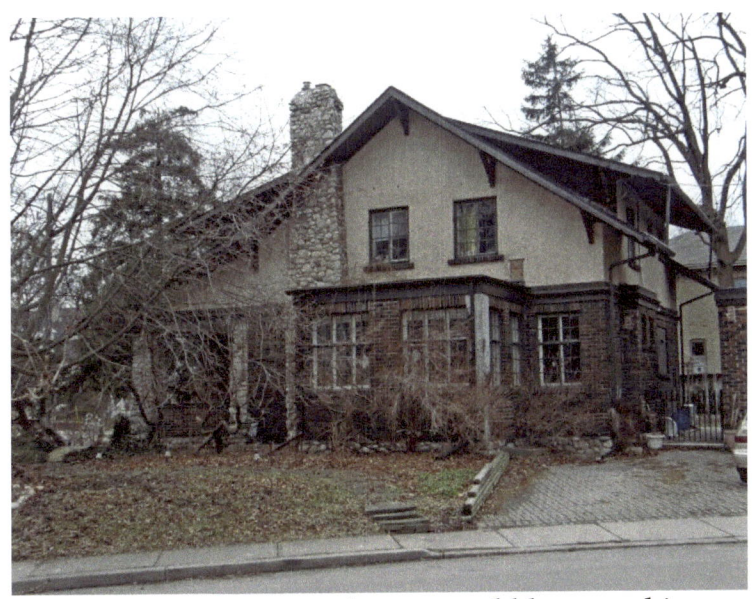

Stucco exterior on second storey, cobblestone chimney

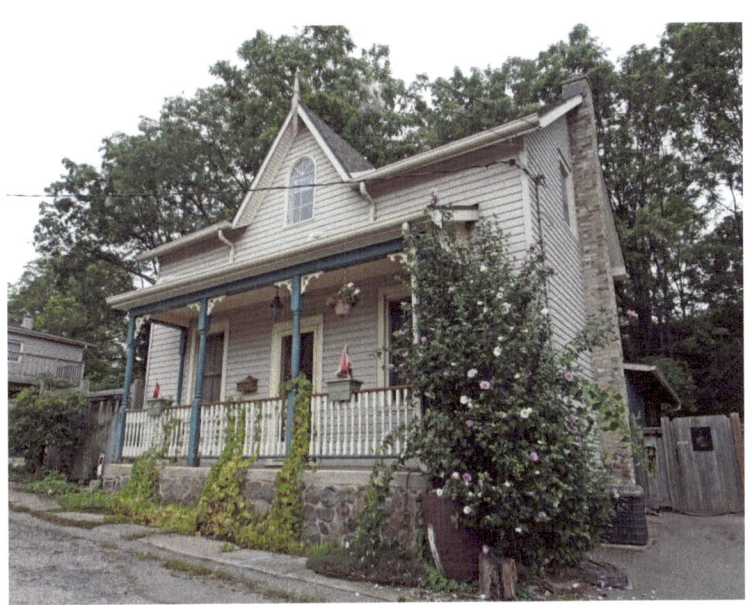

River Lane – Gothic – finial on gable

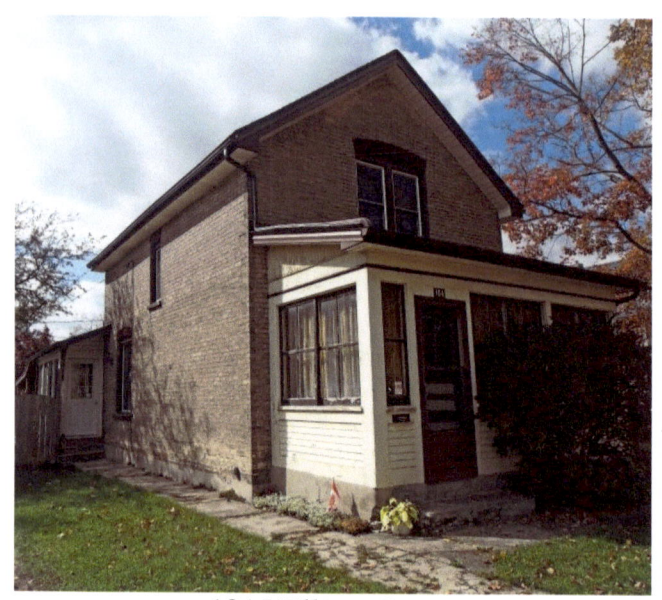

104 William Street

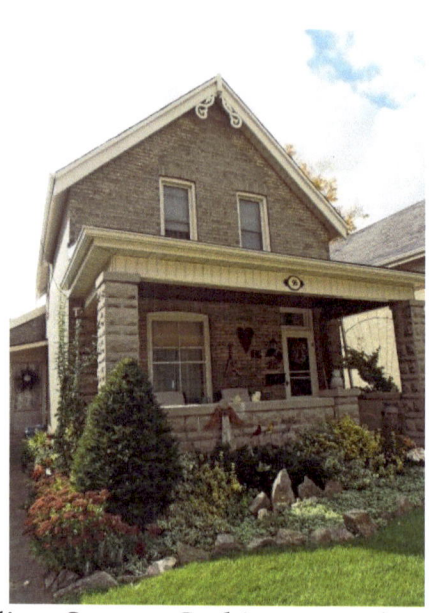

96 William Street – Gothic – verge board trim

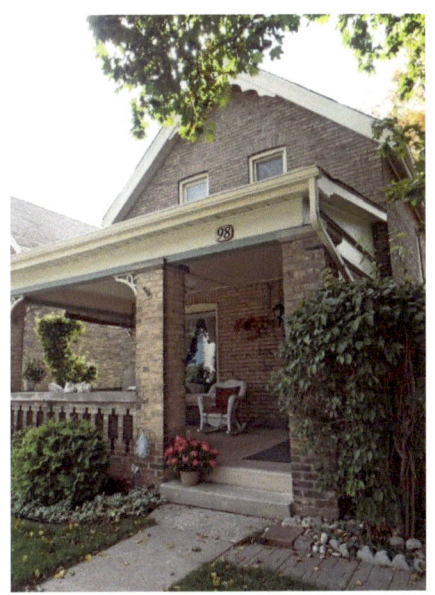

98 William Street

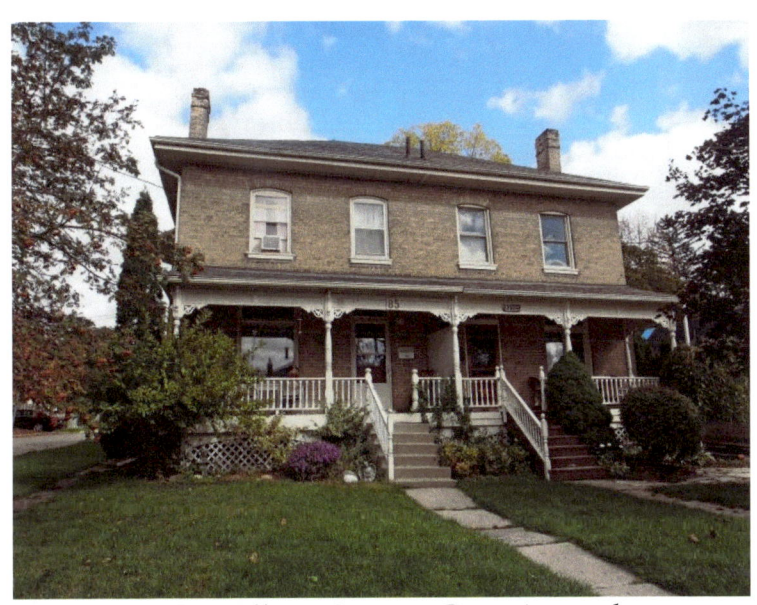

83, 85 William Street – Georgian style

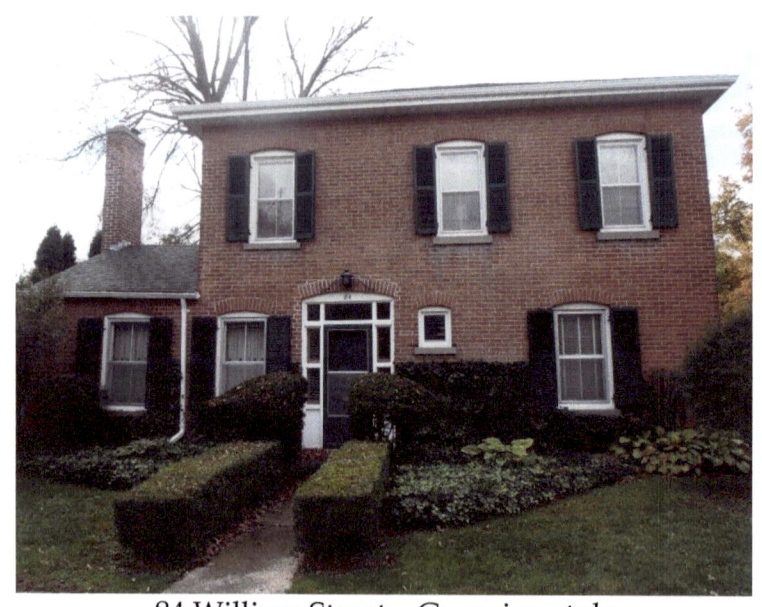

84 William Street – Georgian style

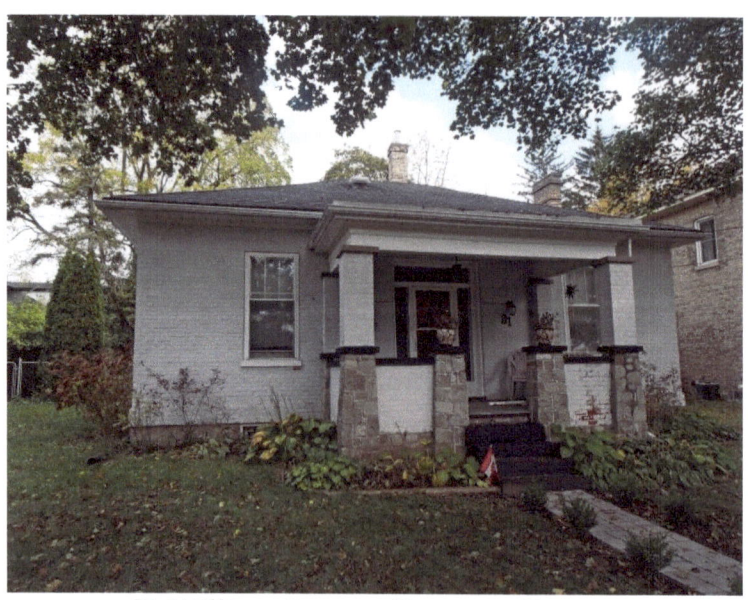

81 William Street – Regency Cottage

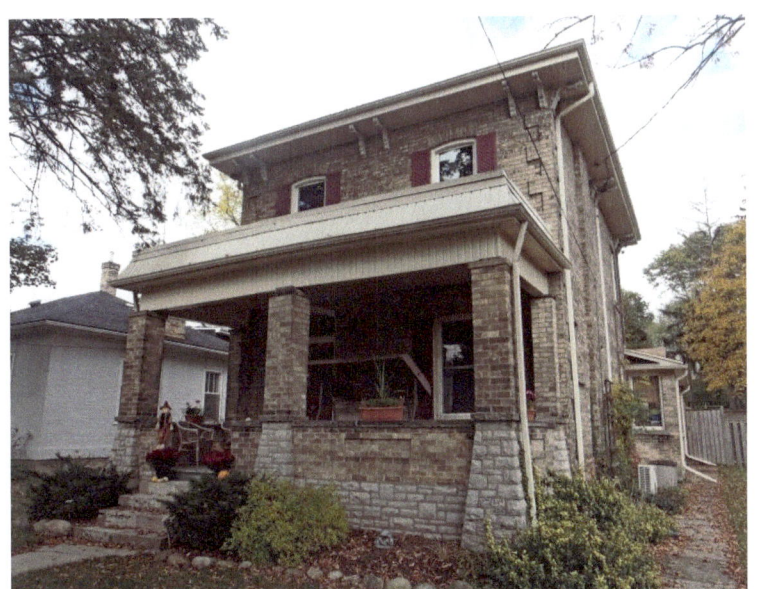

79 William Street – Italianate style – paired cornice brackets,

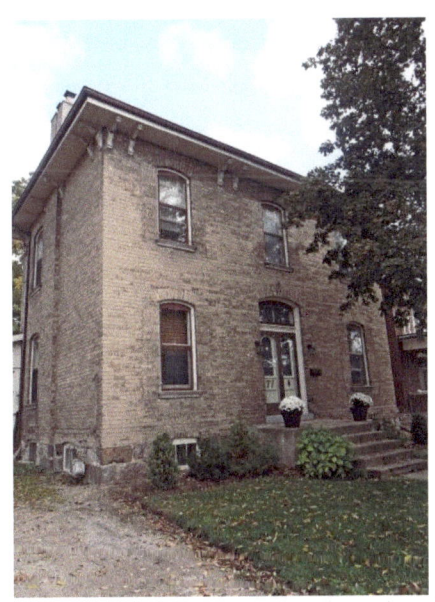

77 William Street – Italianate style, yellow brick, hipped roof, cornice brackets

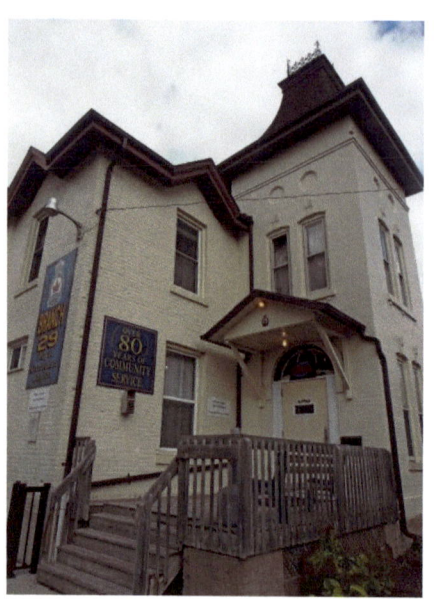

70 William Street – Branch 29 Royal Canadian Legion – two storey tower with iron cresting on roof top

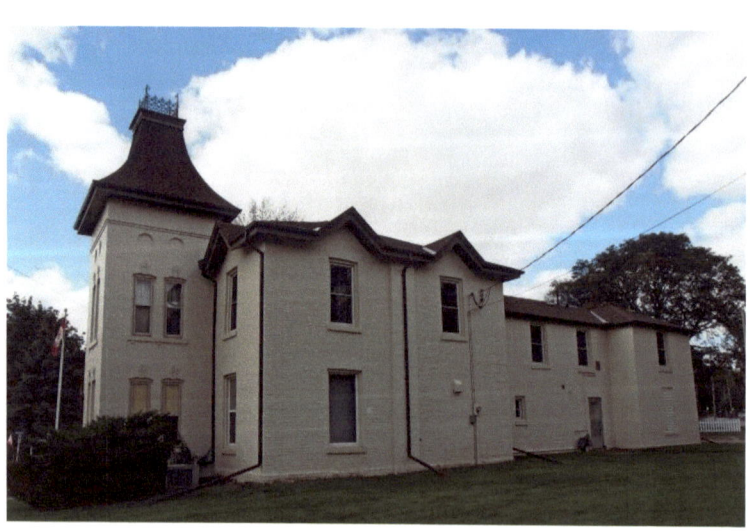

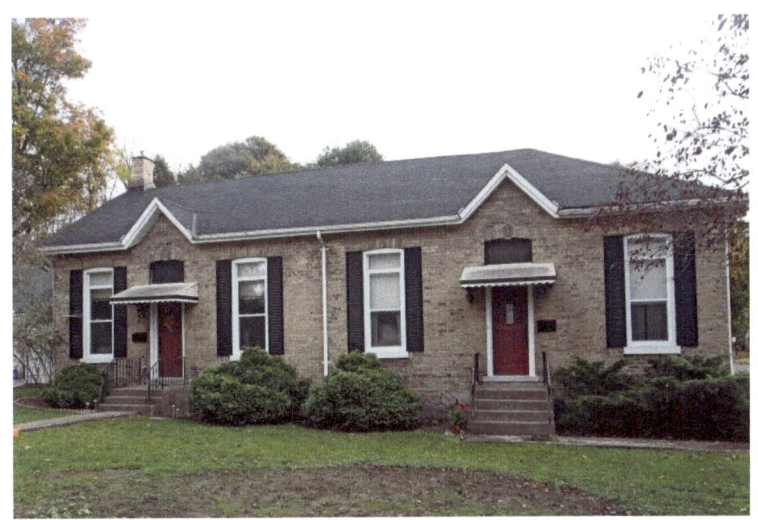

73, 75 William Street – Gothic Revival Cottage

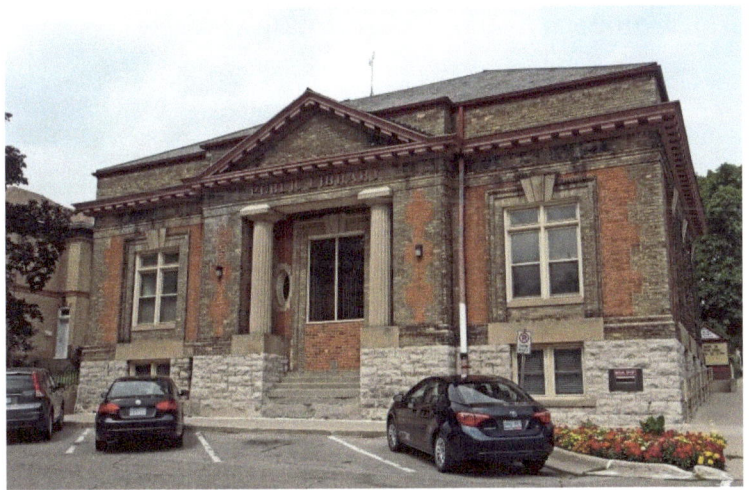

12 William Street - Public Library – built in 1904 with the help of a grant from American philanthropist Andrew Carnegie – dichromatic brickwork, pillars at entrance with pediment above, keystones

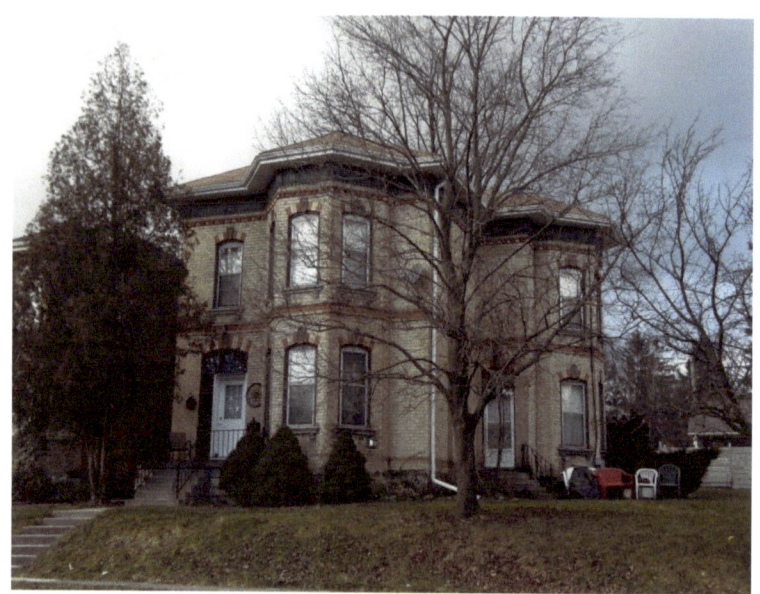

William Street - Italianate style – dichromatic brickwork, banding, two-storey bay windows, hipped roof

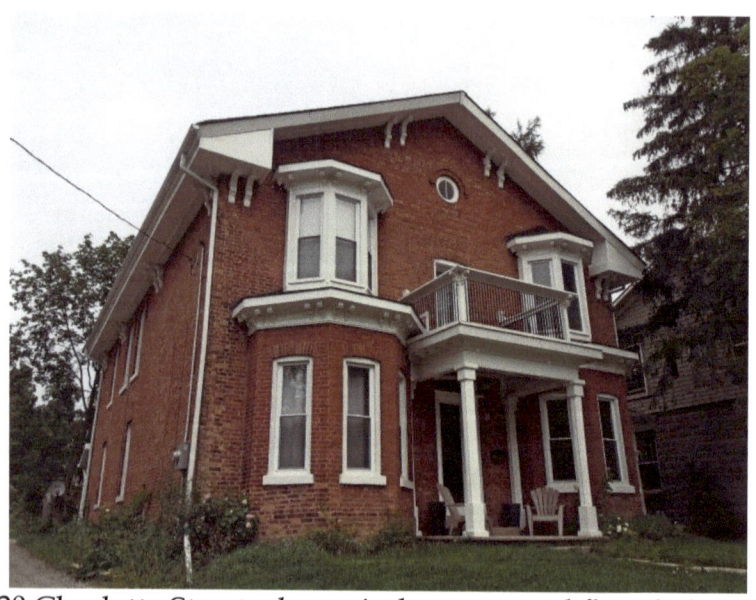

20 Charlotte Street – bay windows, second floor balcony

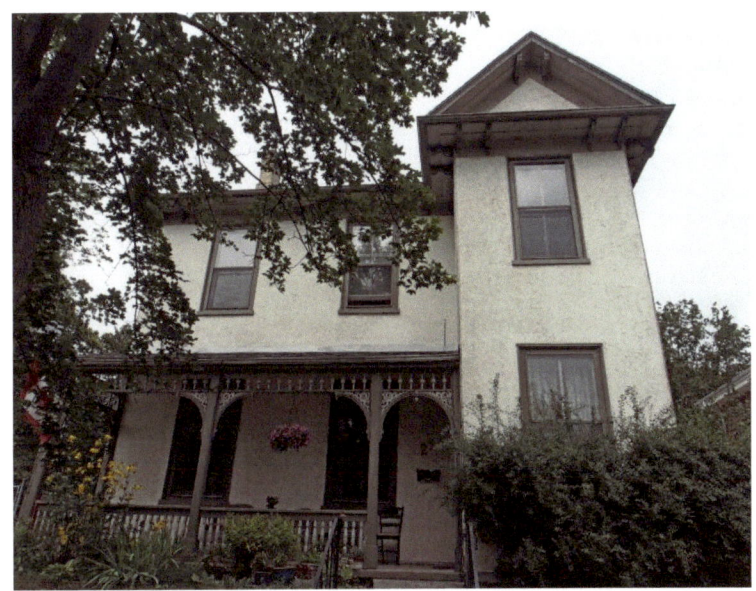

22 Charlotte Street

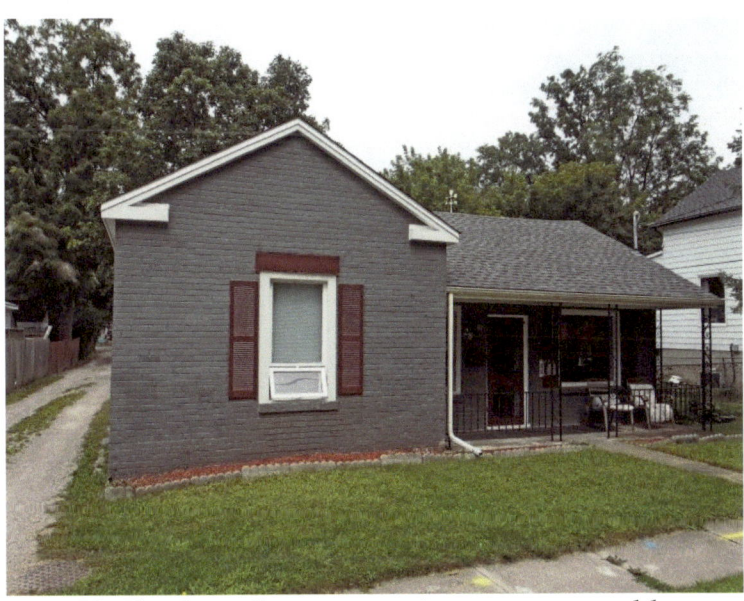

28 Charlotte Street – cornice return on gable

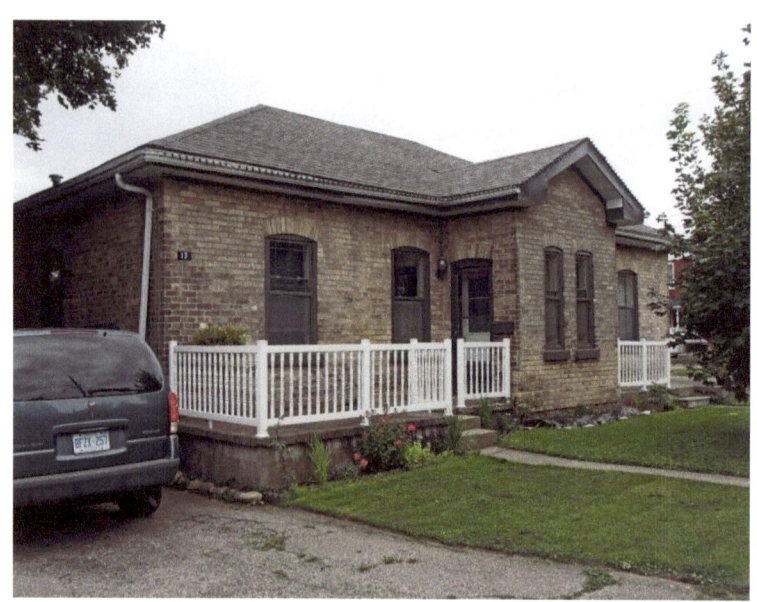

13 Emily Street – Ontario Cottage

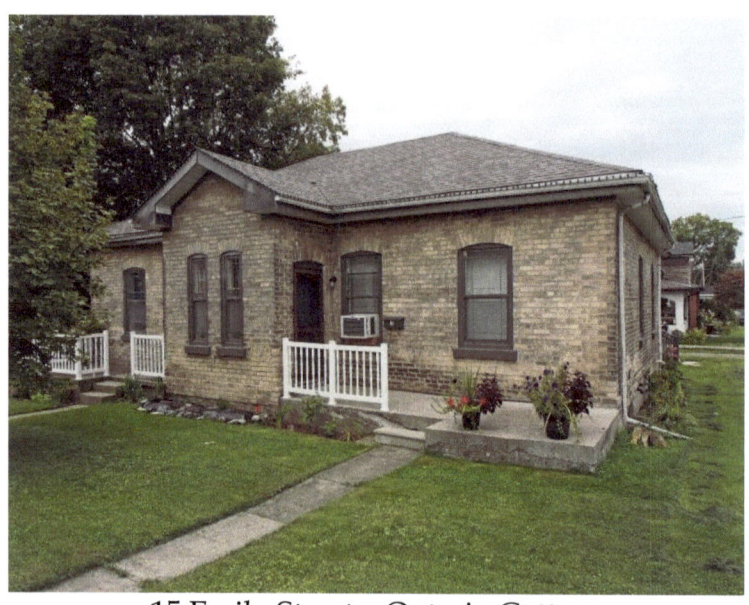

15 Emily Street – Ontario Cottage

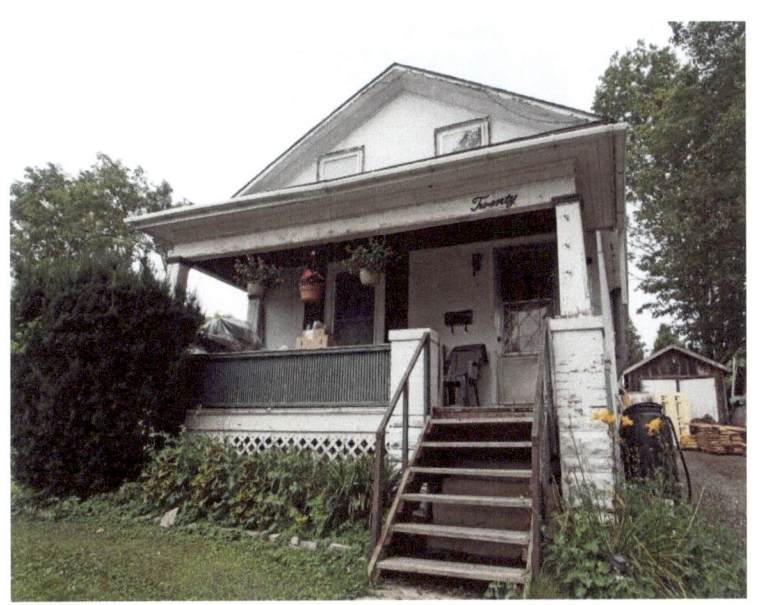

20 Emily Street

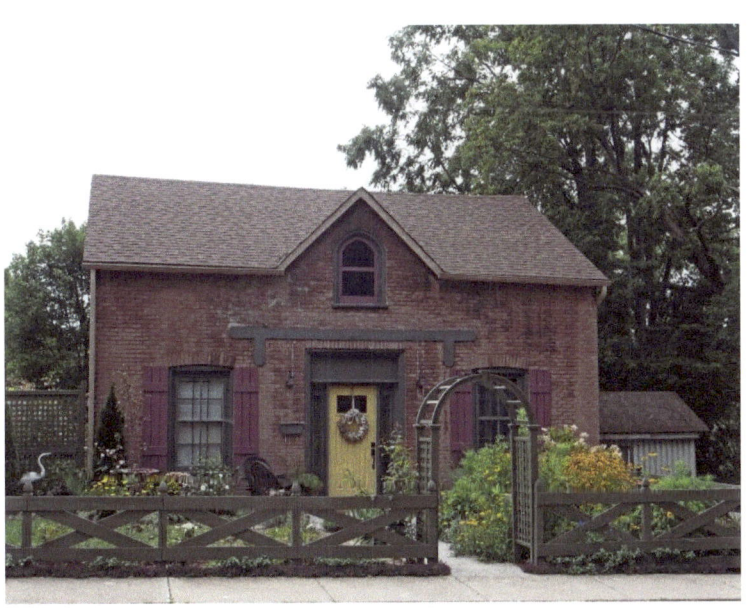

Emily Street – Gothic cottage

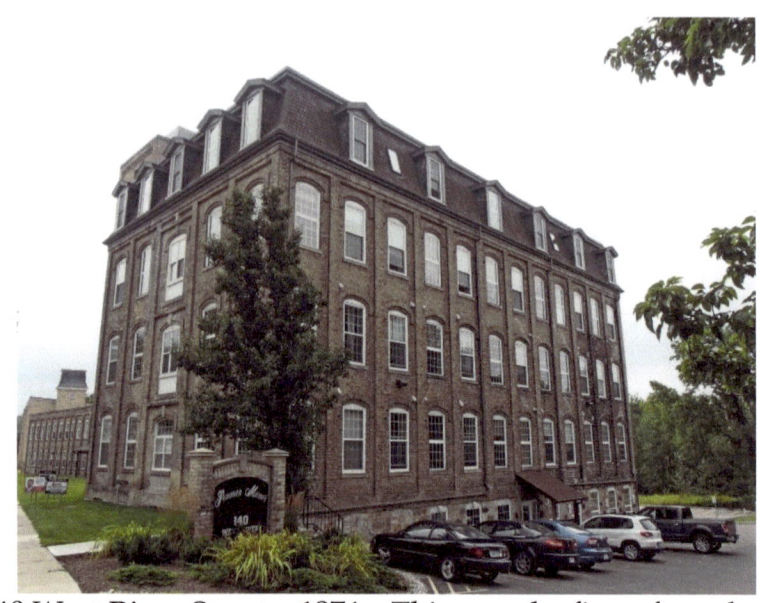

140 West River Street – 1874 – This was the first of two large textile mills built by Paris industrialist John Penman. Dependent on waterpower in the beginning, a generating plant still stands behind the mill buildings on the bank of the Nith River.

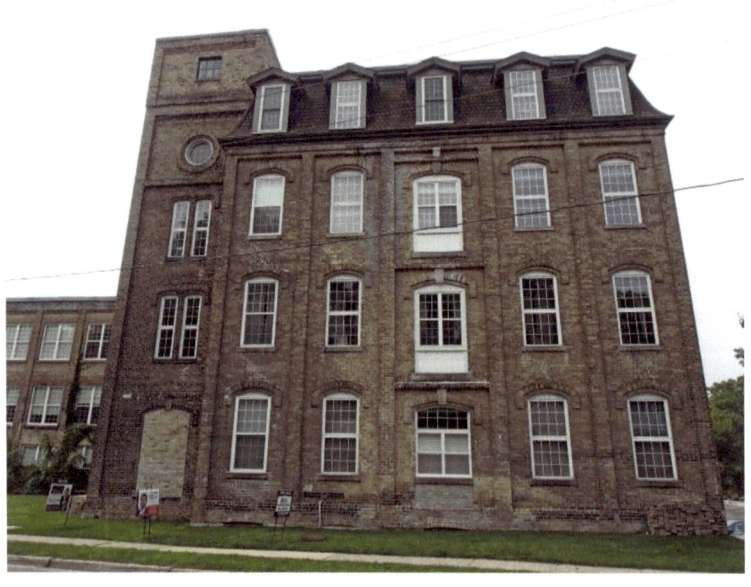

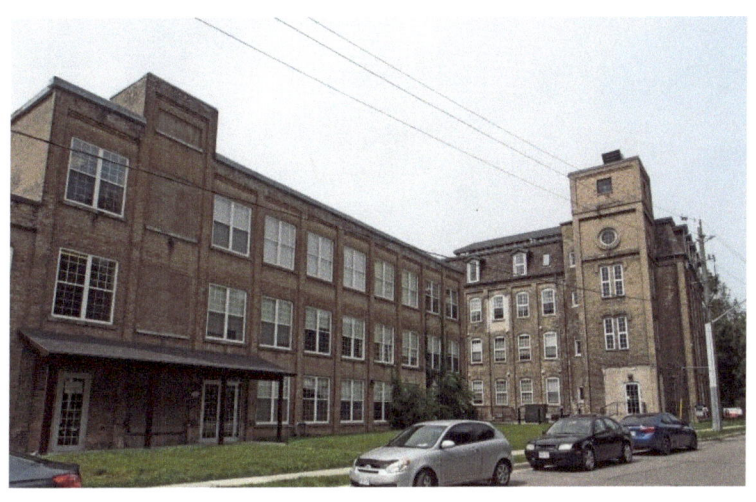

130-140 West River Street

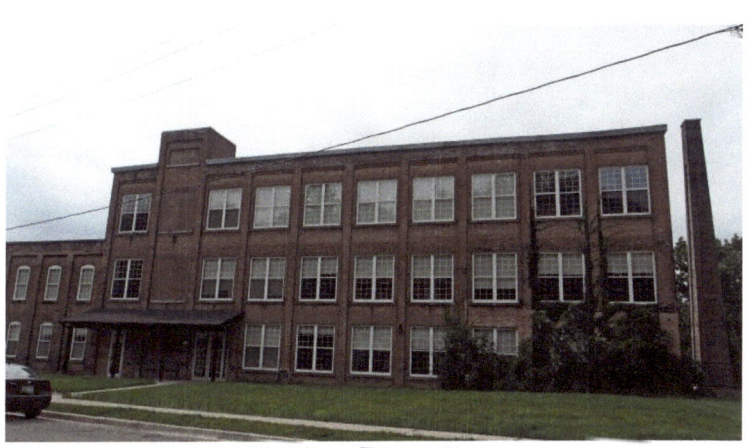

130 West River Street

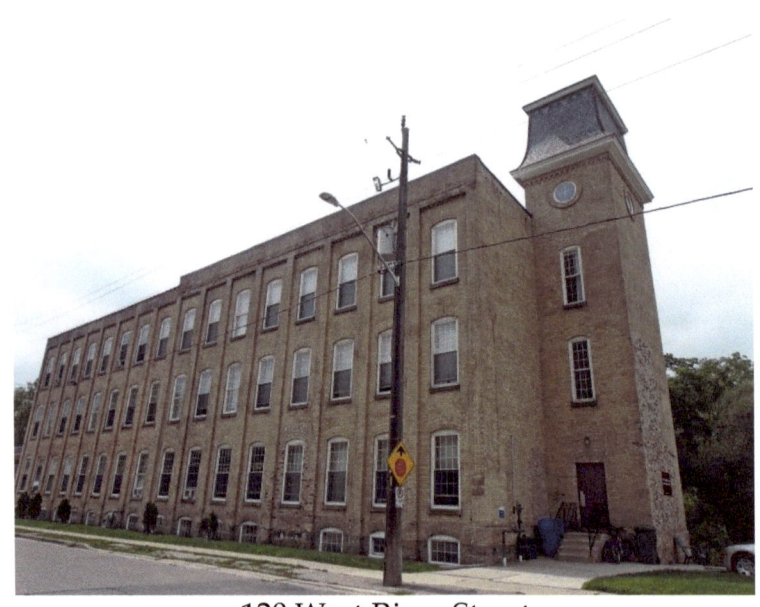
120 West River Street

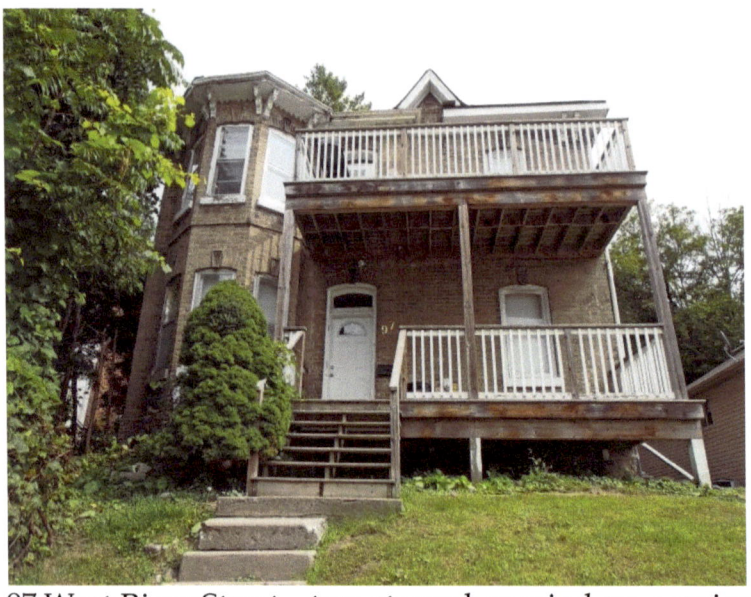
97 West River Street – two-storey bay window, cornice brackets

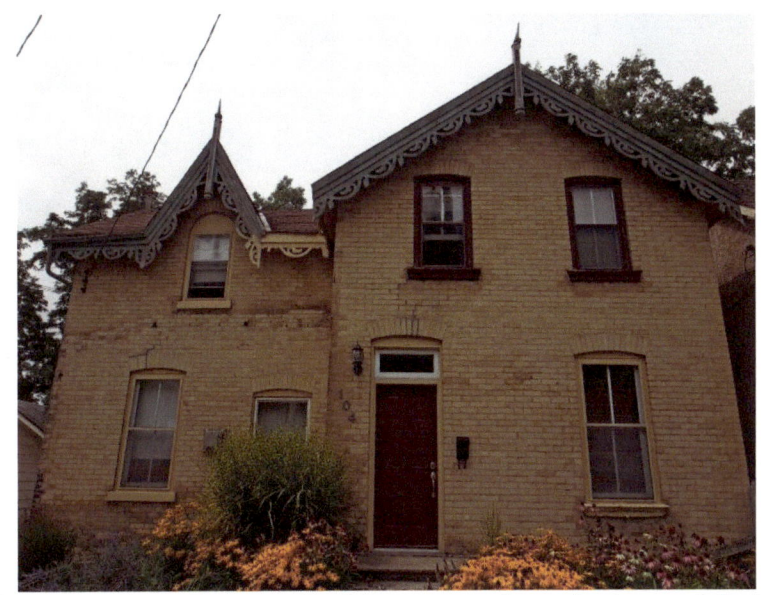

104 West River Street – Gothic – verge board trim and finials on gables

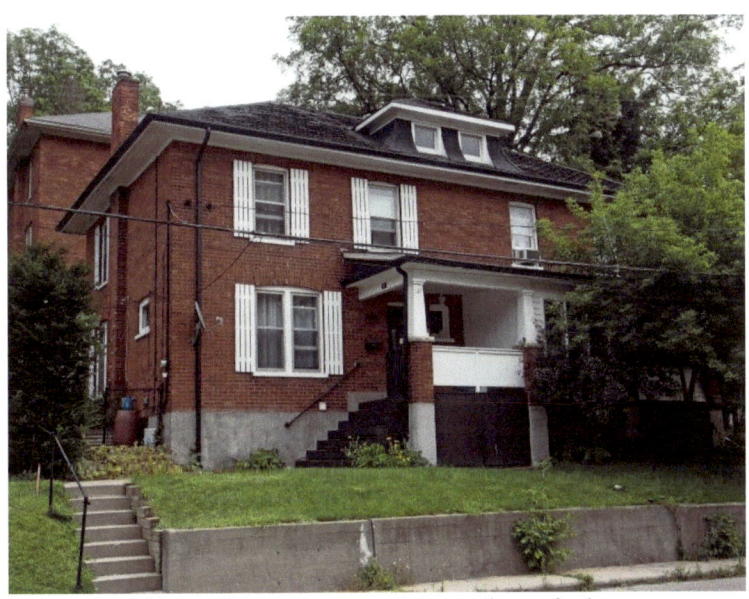

107 West River Street – hipped roof, dormer

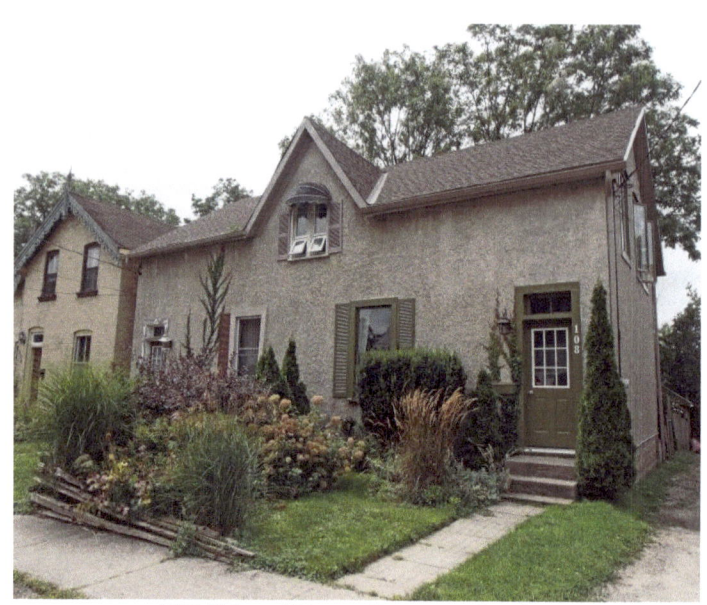

108 West River Street - Gothic

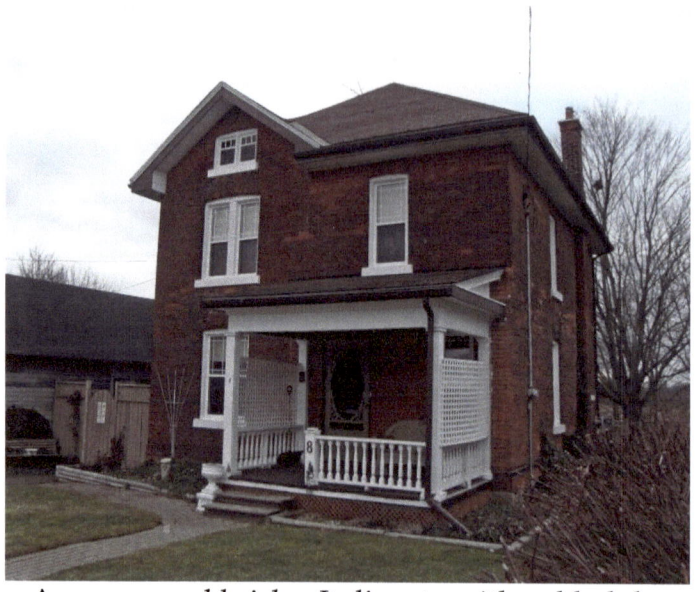

8 John Avenue – red brick – Italianate with gabled dormer in attic

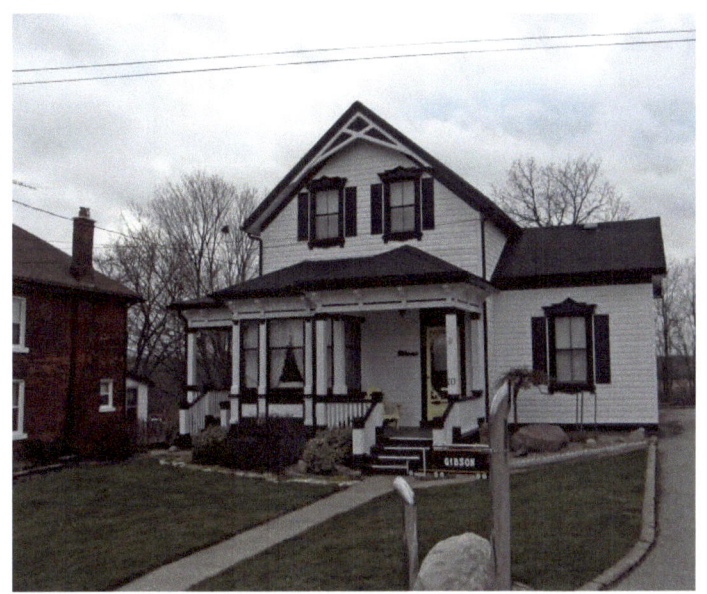

10 John Avenue – decorative verge board on Gothic style gable, verandah with cornice brackets

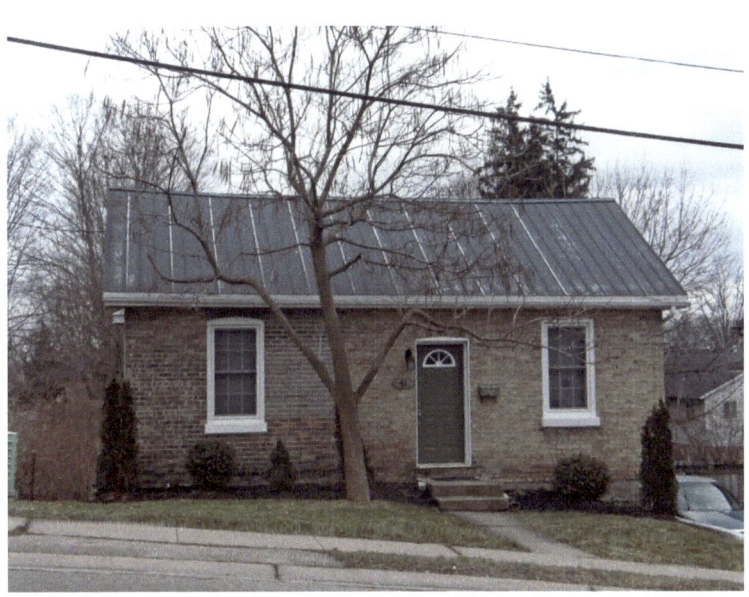

41 John Avenue – Ontario Cottage

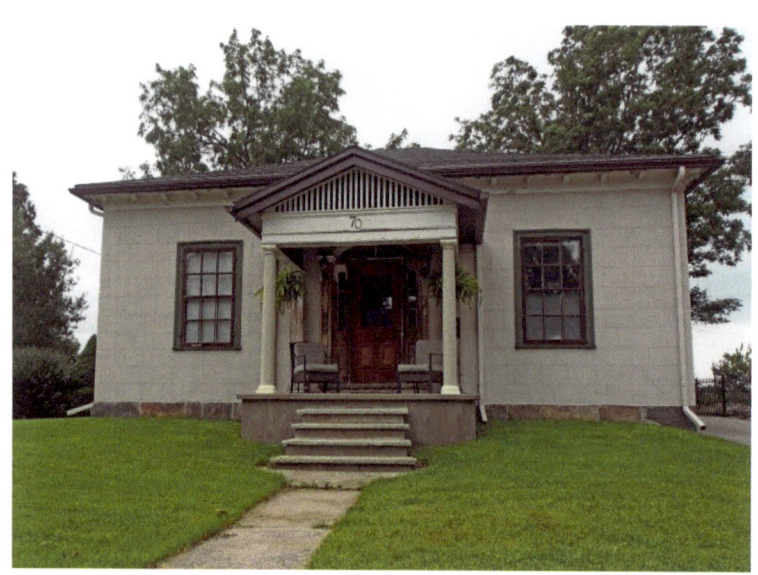
70 Banfield Street

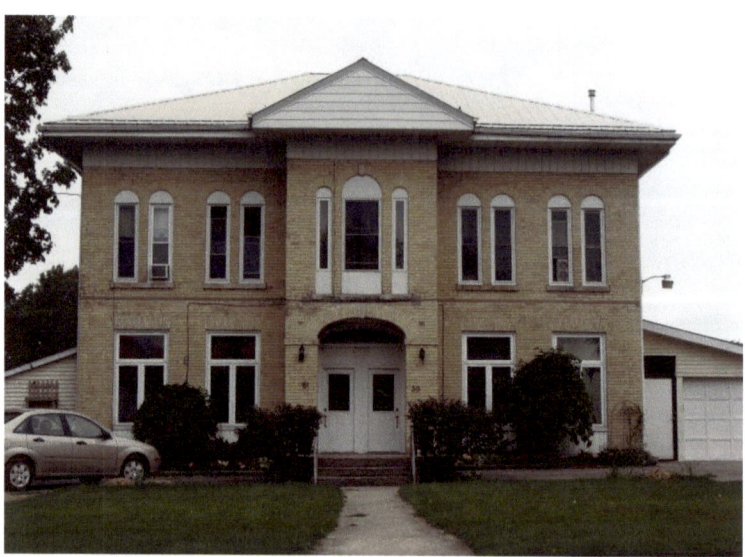
59-61 Banfield Street – Georgian – two-storey frontispiece with pediment

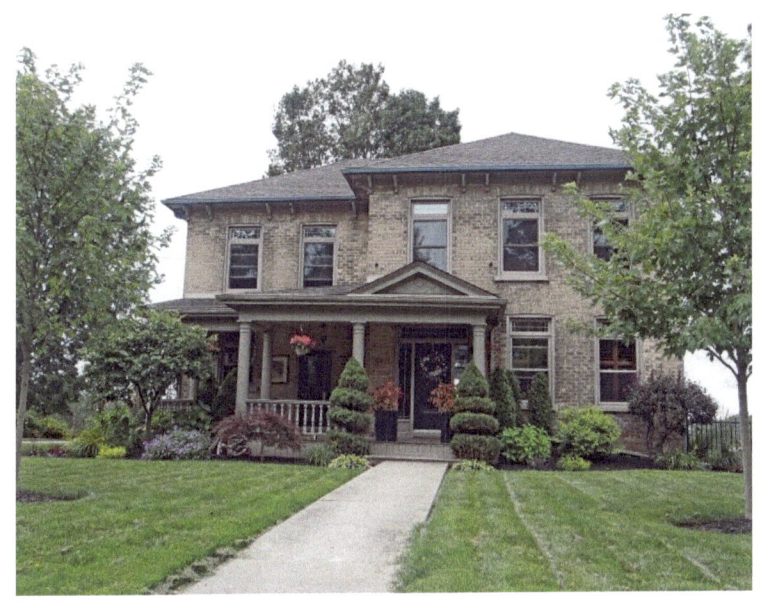

66 Banfield Street - hipped roof, cornice brackets, pediment

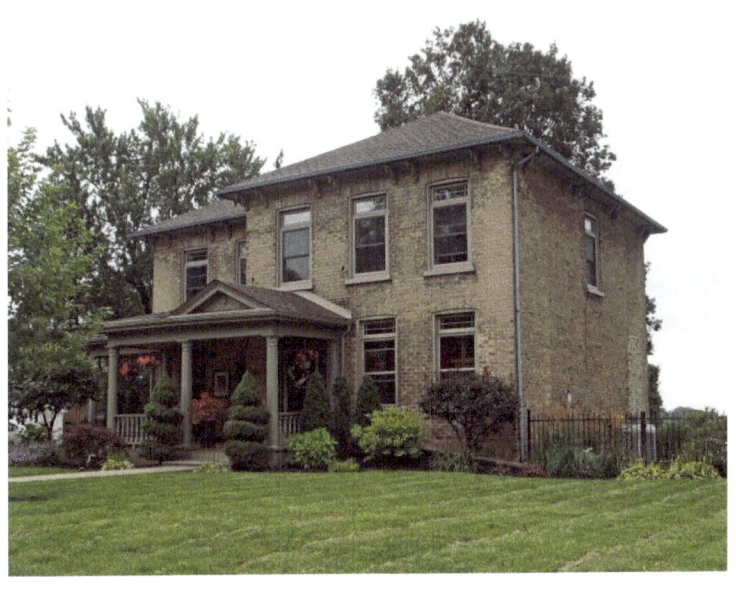

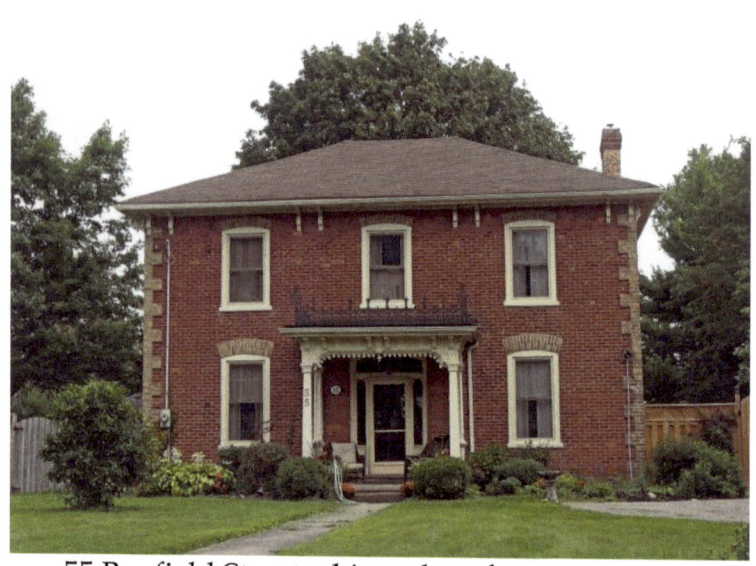
55 Banfield Street – hipped roof, corner quoins

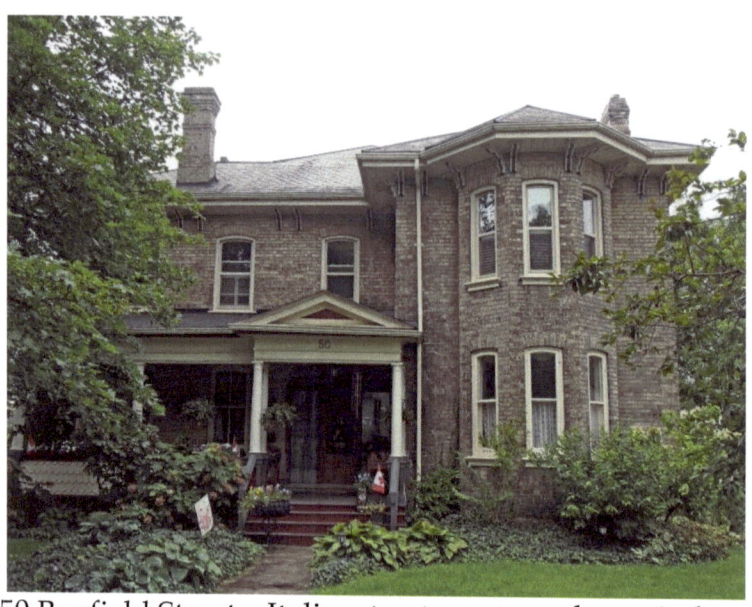
50 Banfield Street – Italianate - two-storey bay window, cornice brackets, pediment

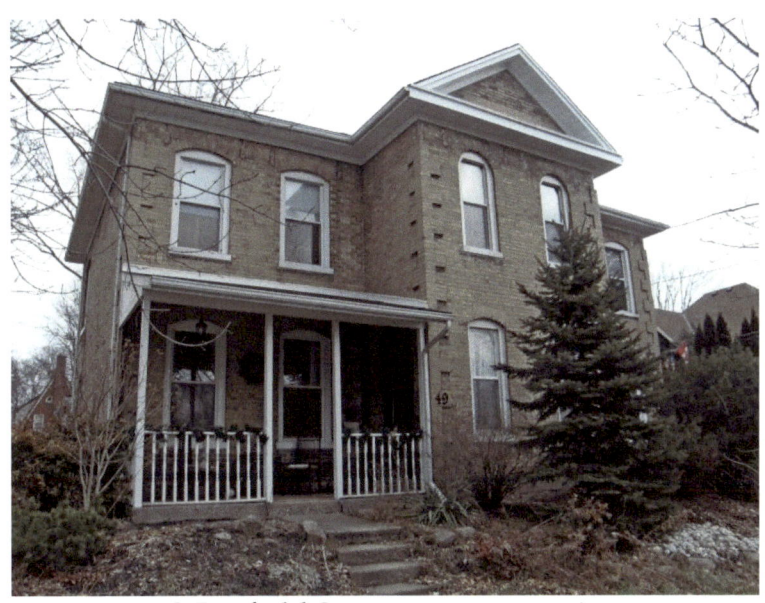

49 Banfield Street – corner quoins

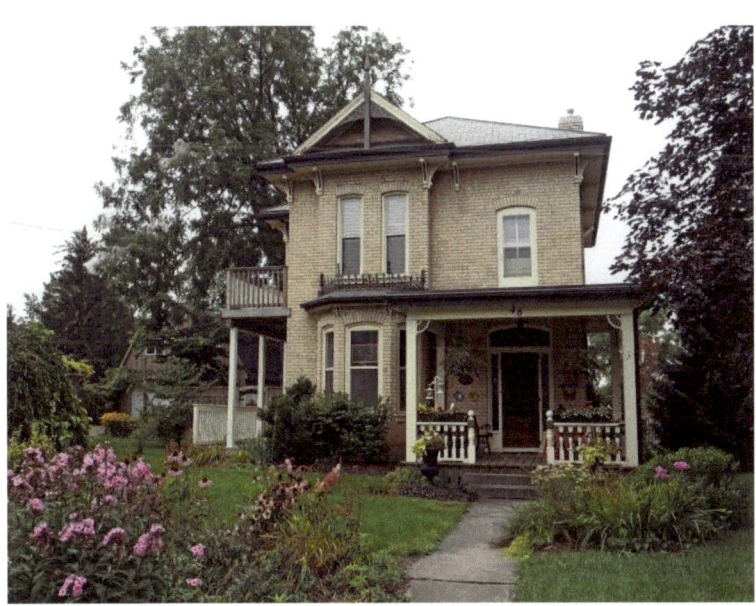

48 Banfield Street – Italianate - bay window with iron cresting above

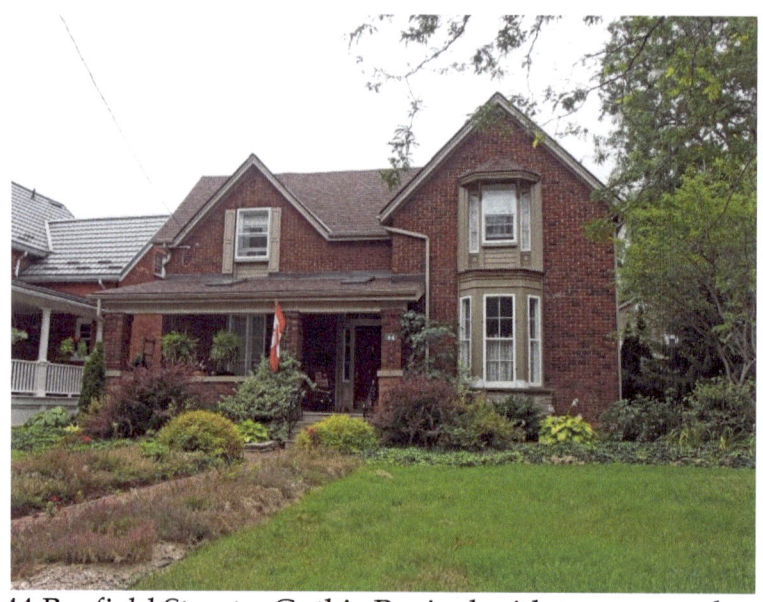

44 Banfield Street – Gothic Revival with two-storey bay windows; red brick

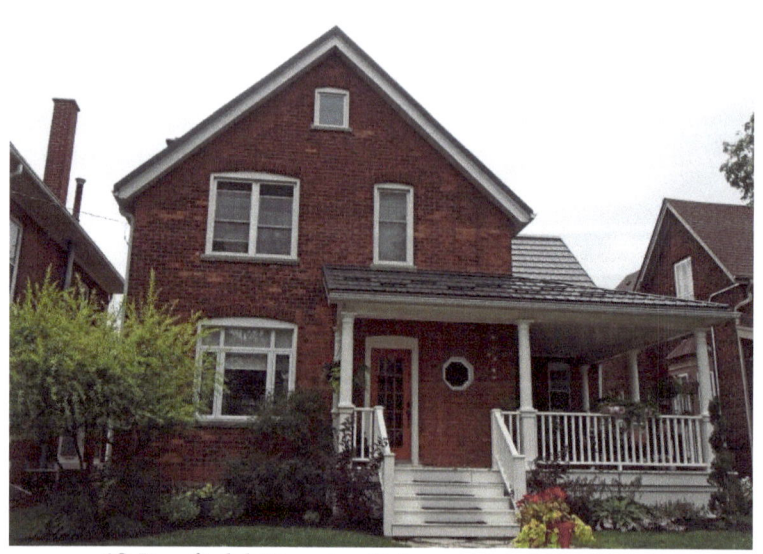

42 Banfield Street – Edwardian, red brick

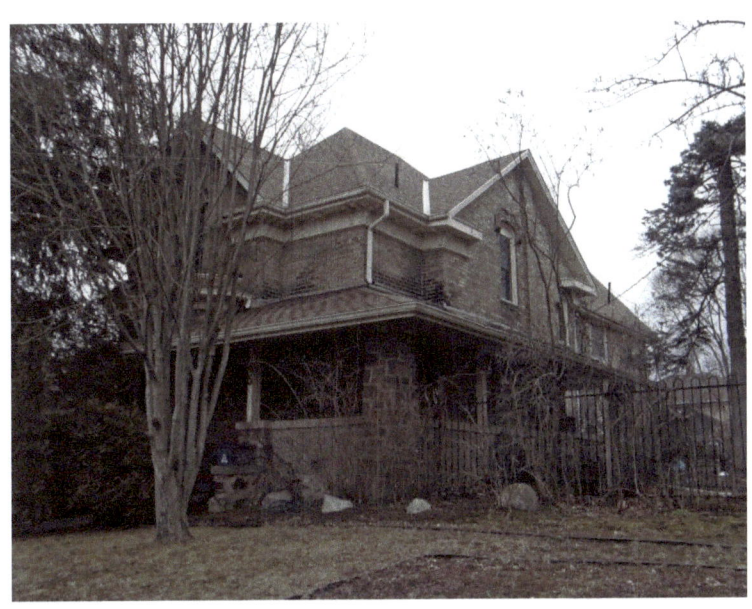

Banfield Street –Queen Anne style – yellow brick

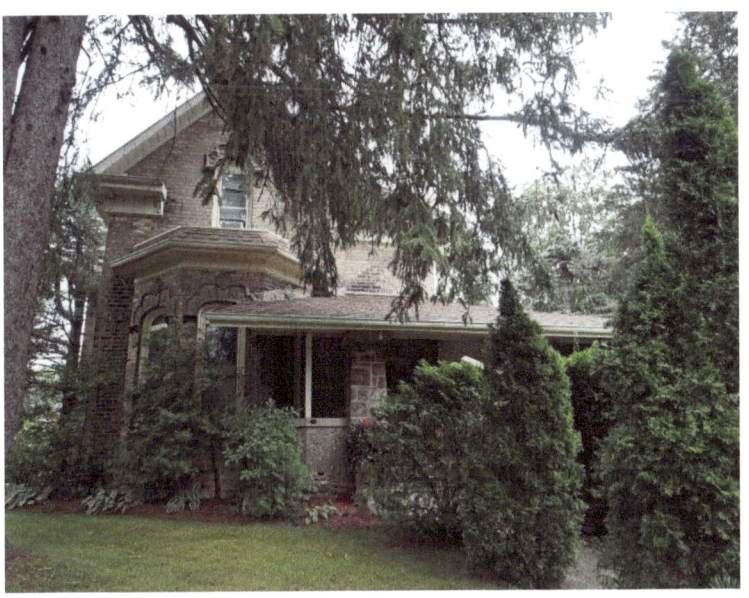

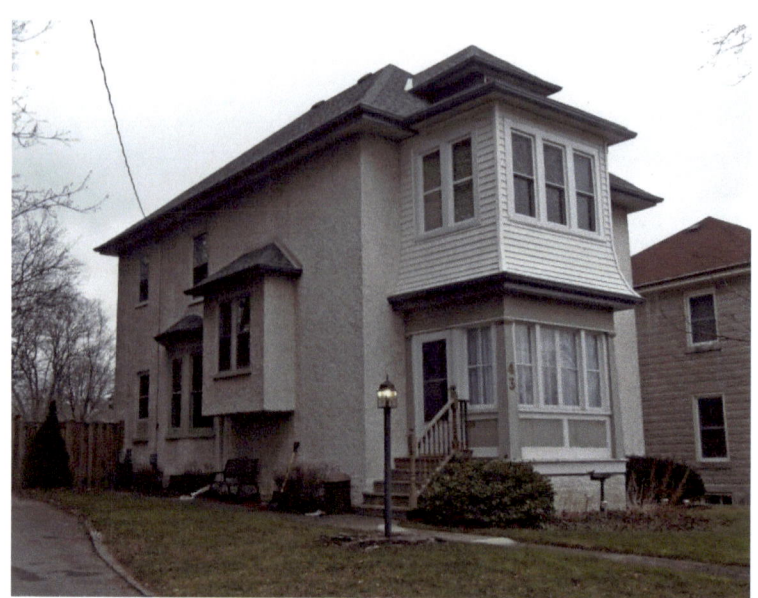

43 Banfield Street – stucco exterior

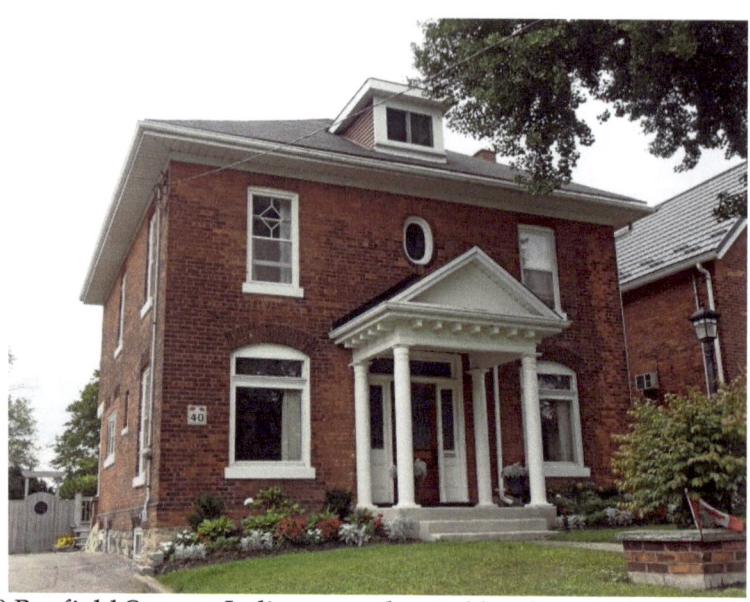

40 Banfield Street – Italianate style - red brick, round window in centre of second storey, dormer in the attic, pediment above porch

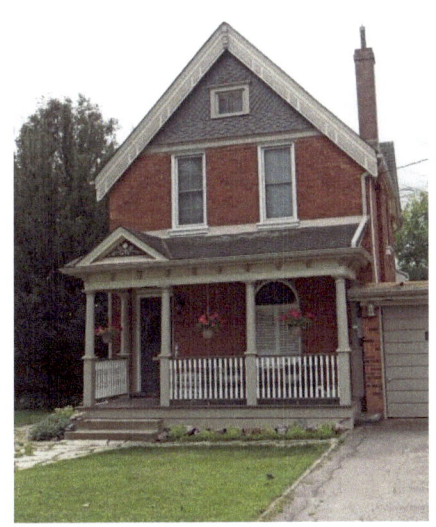

38 Banfield Street – Edwardian – pediment with decorated tympanum

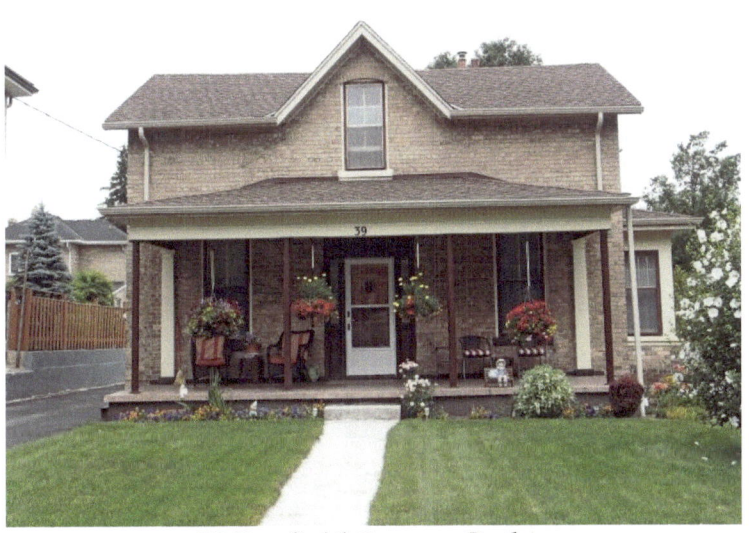

39 Banfield Street - Gothic

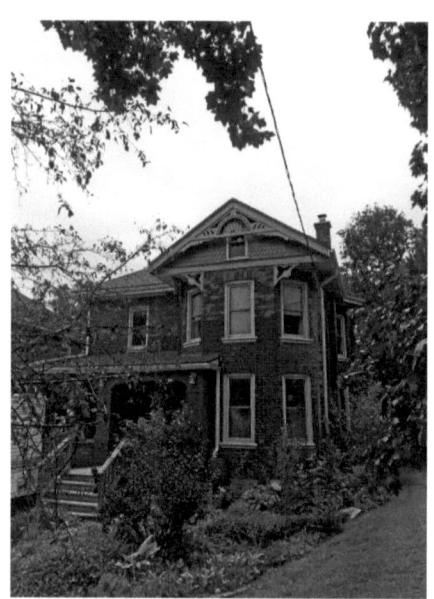

36 Banfield Street – Italianate/Gothic Revival – hip roof, cornice brackets, two-storey bay window with decorative verge board on gable, voussoirs above windows

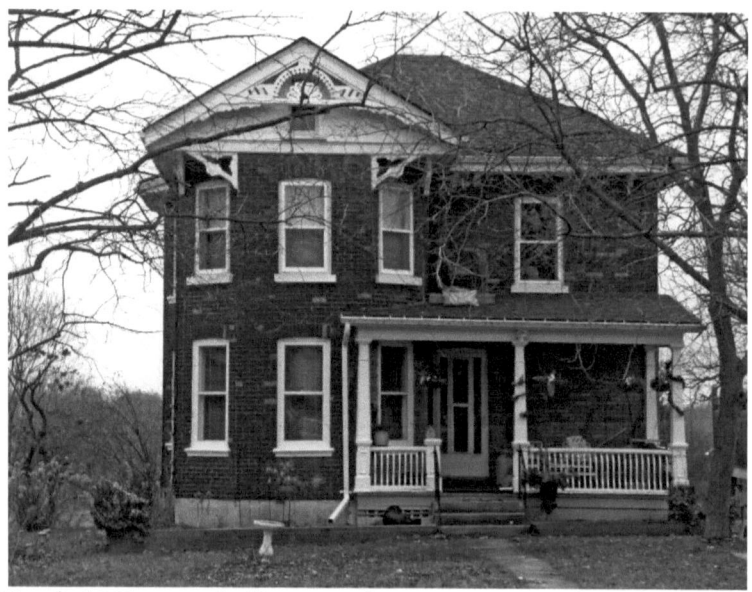

Banfield Street – Italianate – decorative verge board, cornice brackets

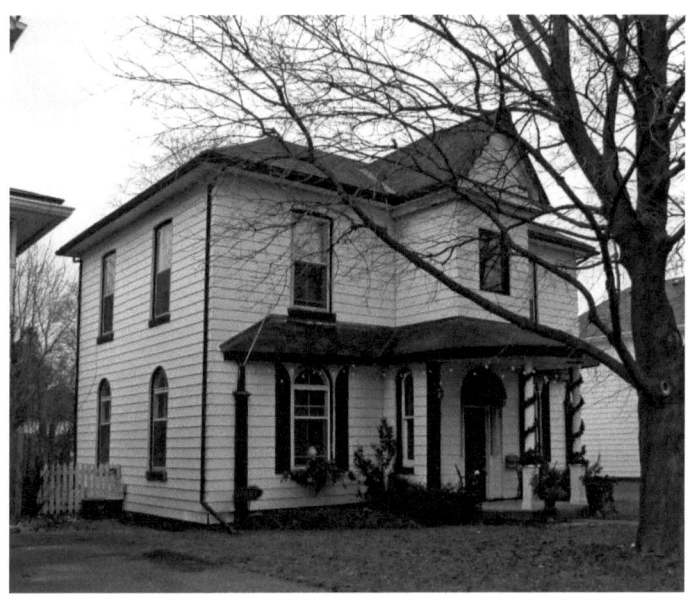

Banfield Street

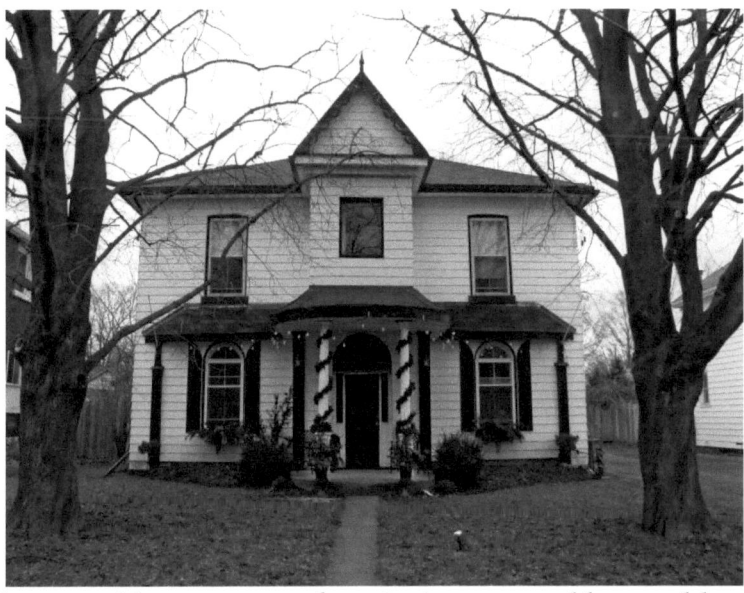

Italianate with two-storey frontispiece topped by a gable with decorative verge boards and finial

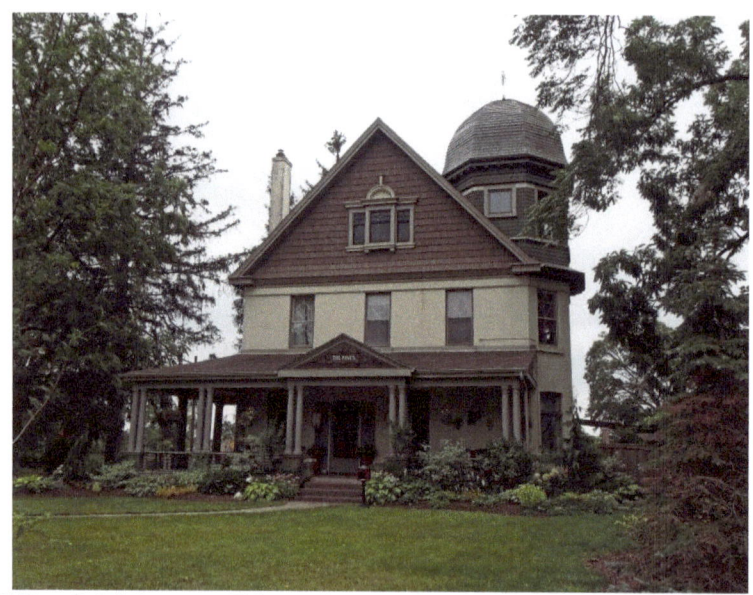

18 Banfield Street – Edwardian style – Palladian window, turret extending through the roof

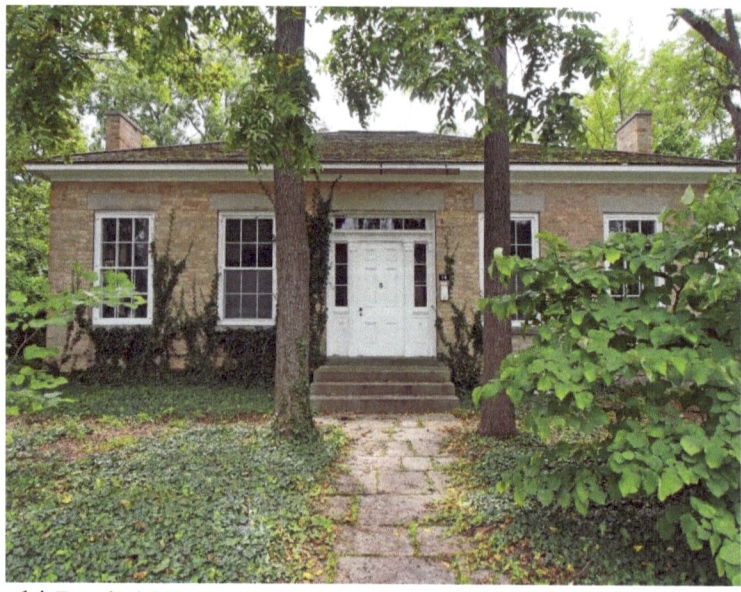

14 Banfield Street – Ontario Cottage – sidelights, transom

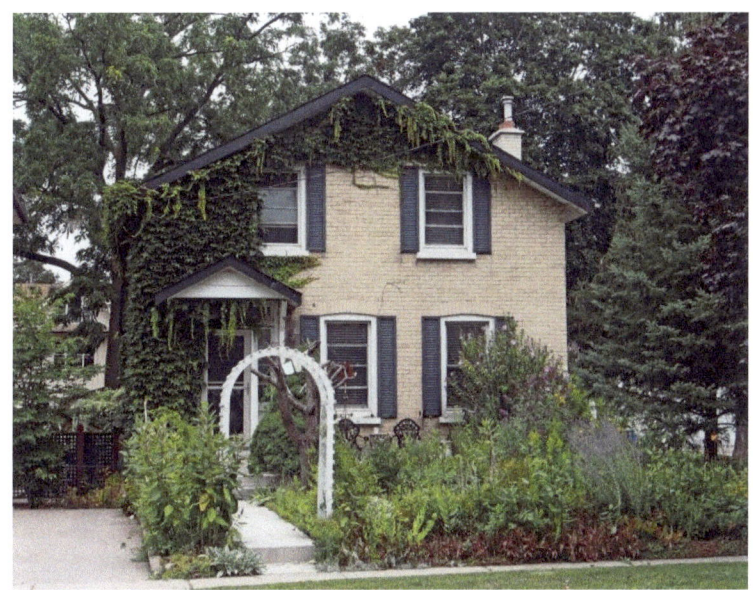

Banfield Street - Gothic

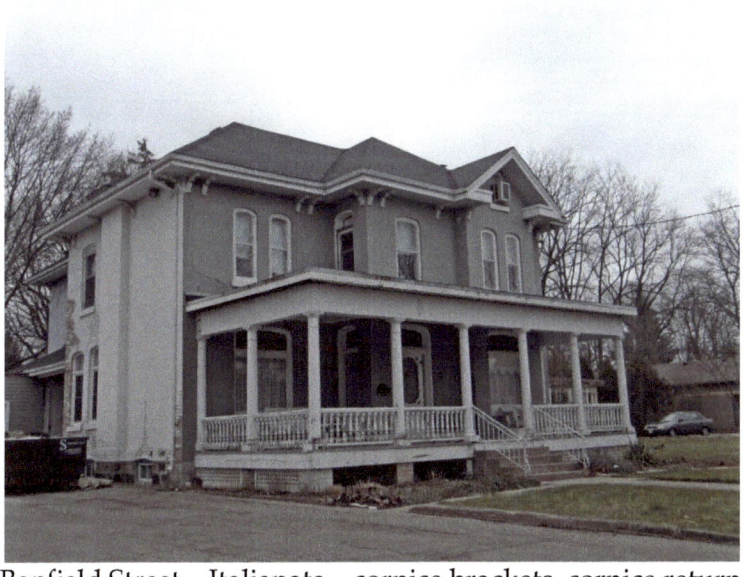

13 Banfield Street – Italianate – cornice brackets, cornice return on gable

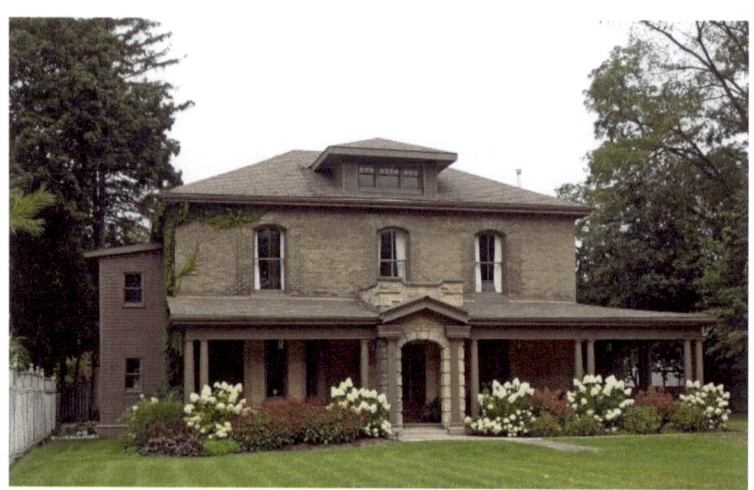

11 Banfield Street – hipped roof with dormer

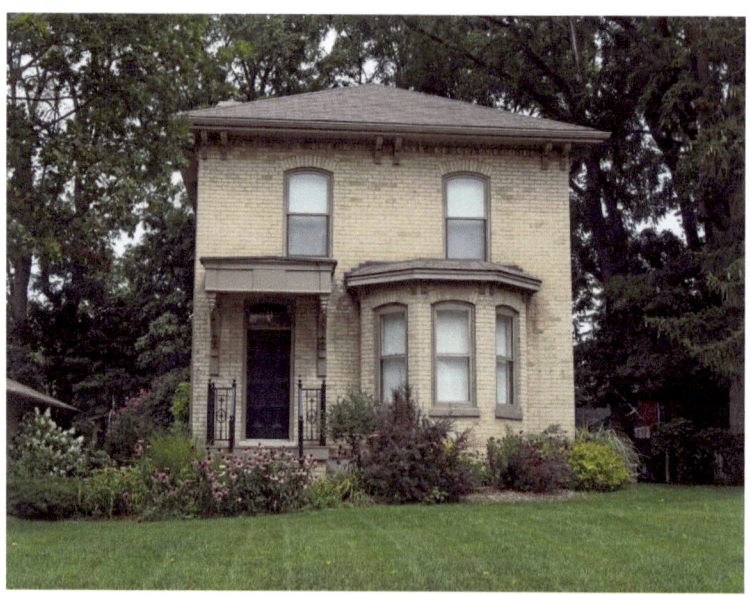

9 Banfield Street – hipped roof, paired cornice brackets, bay window

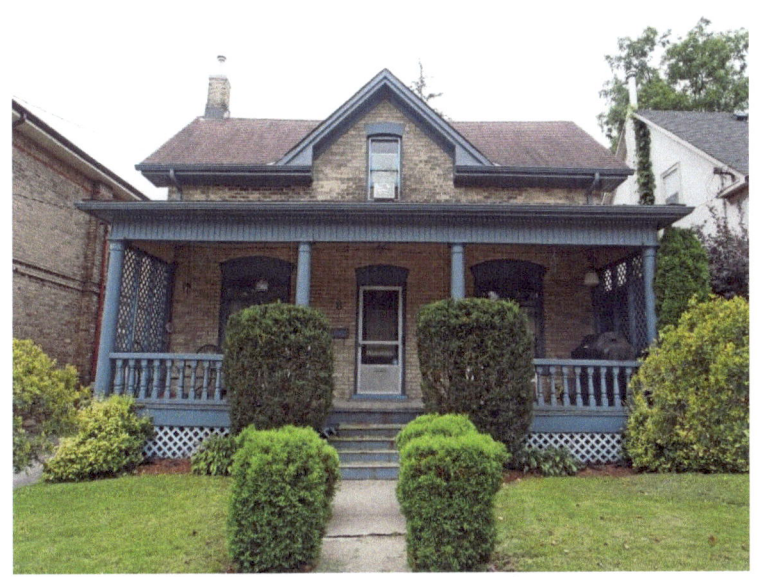

8 Banfield Street - Gothic

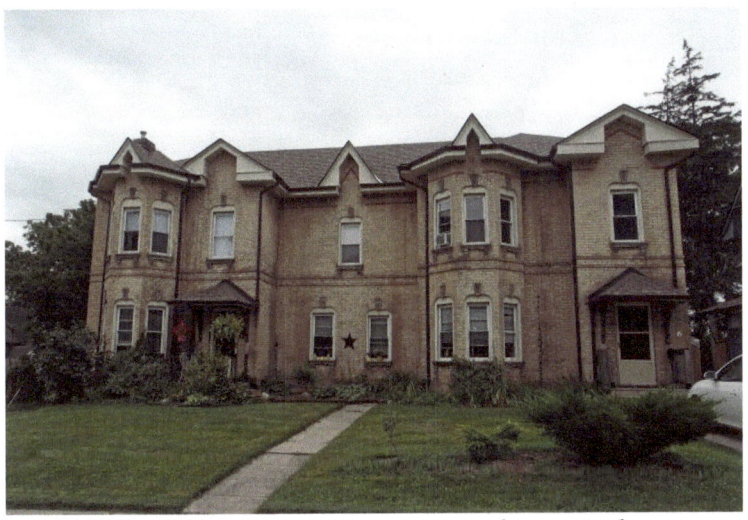

4-6 Banfield Street – two-storey bay windows

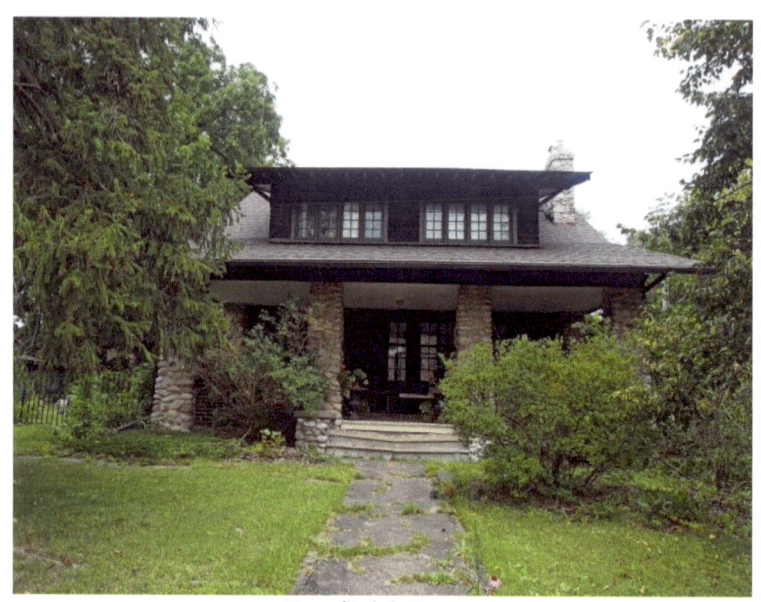

Banfield Street

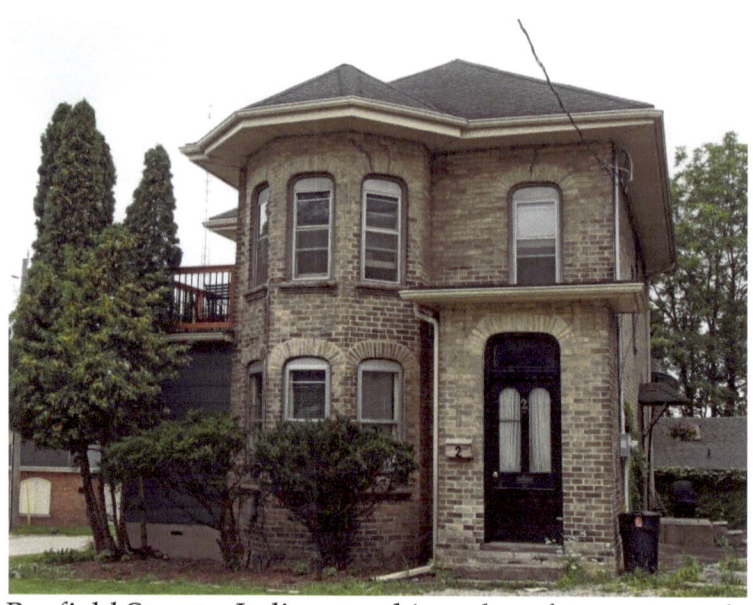

2 Banfield Street – Italianate – hipped roof, two-storey bay window

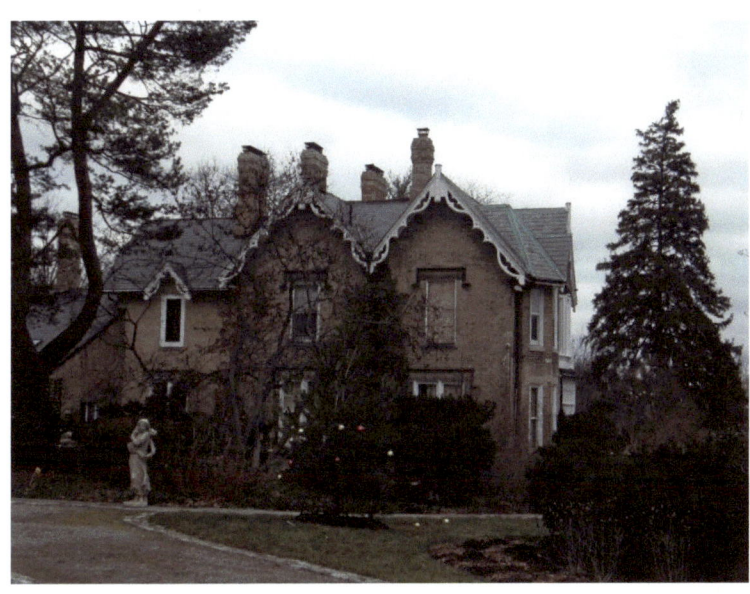

1 Banfield Street – built about 1868 by miller Charles Whitlaw – Gothic Revival – verge board trim on gables, compound chimneys

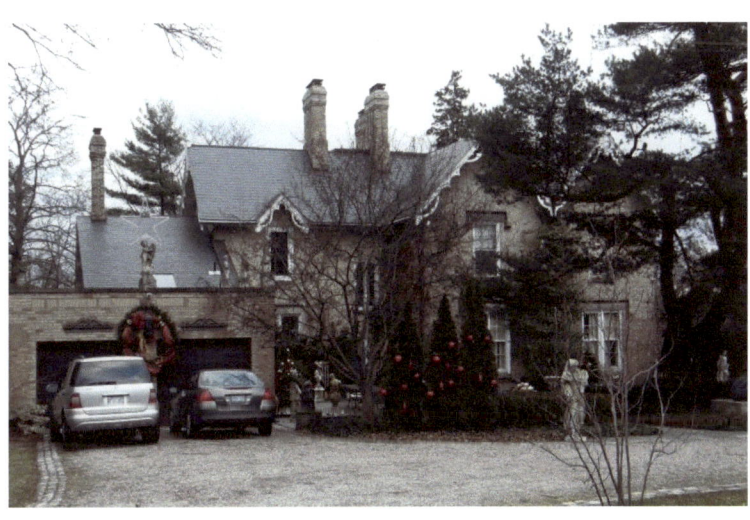

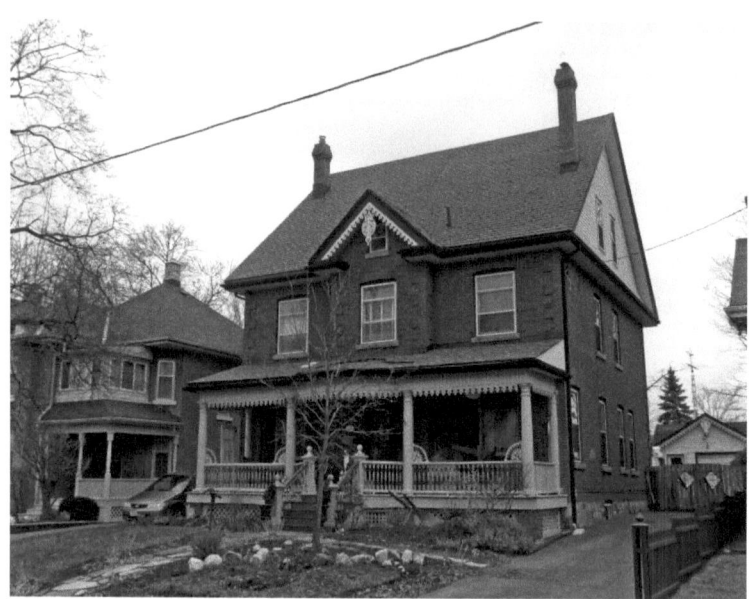

15 Jane Street – Gothic Revival style – verge board trim on gable, central frontispiece

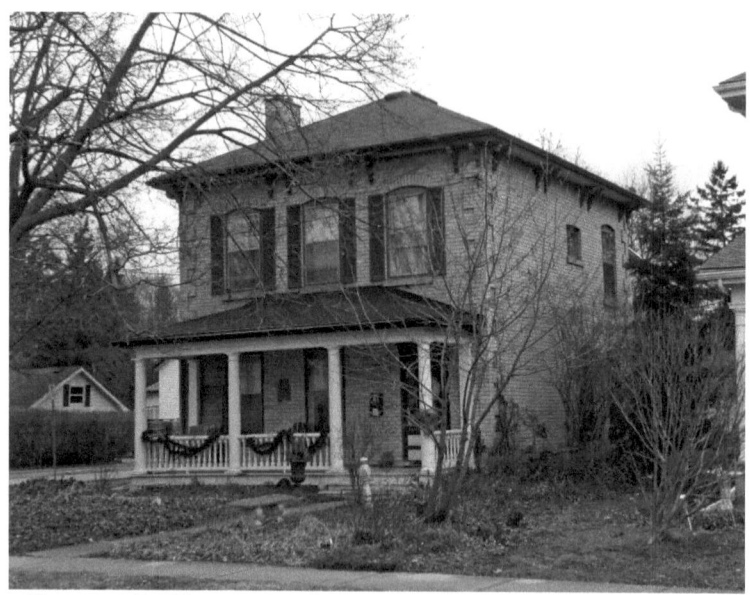

Jane Street – Italianate style – paired cornice brackets, hipped roof

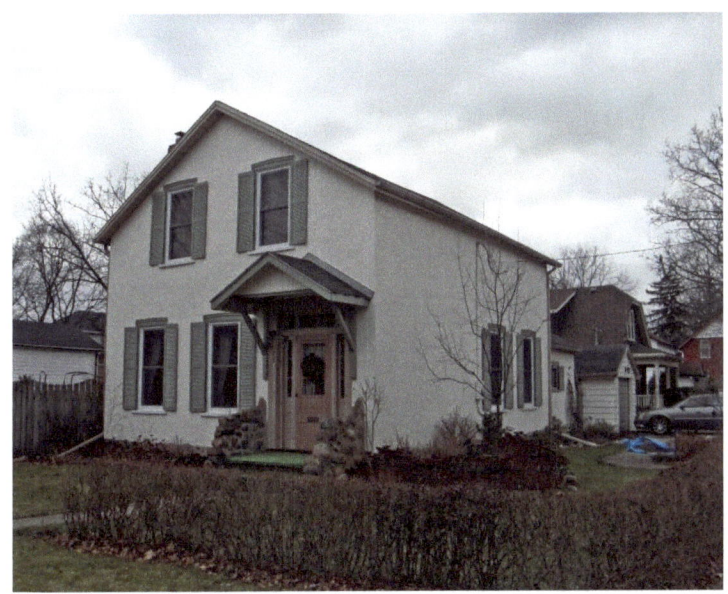

24 Jane Street – 1½ storey Gothic Cottage with stucco exterior

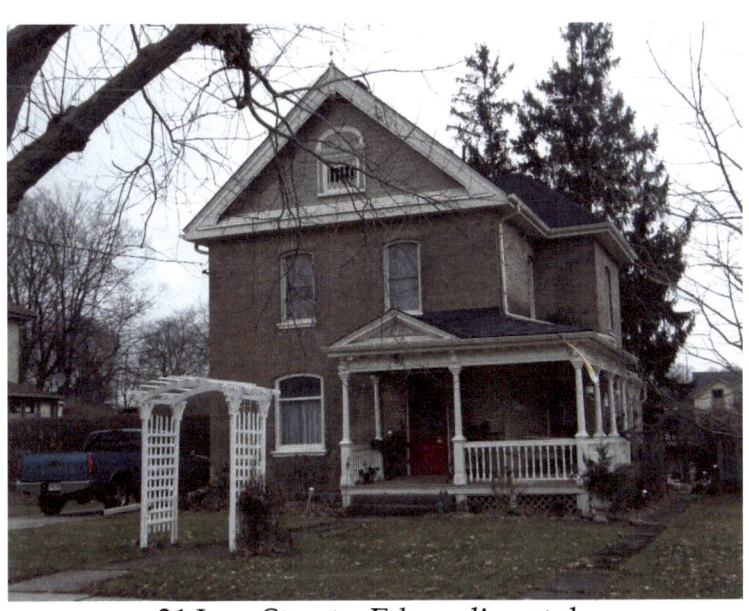

31 Jane Street – Edwardian style

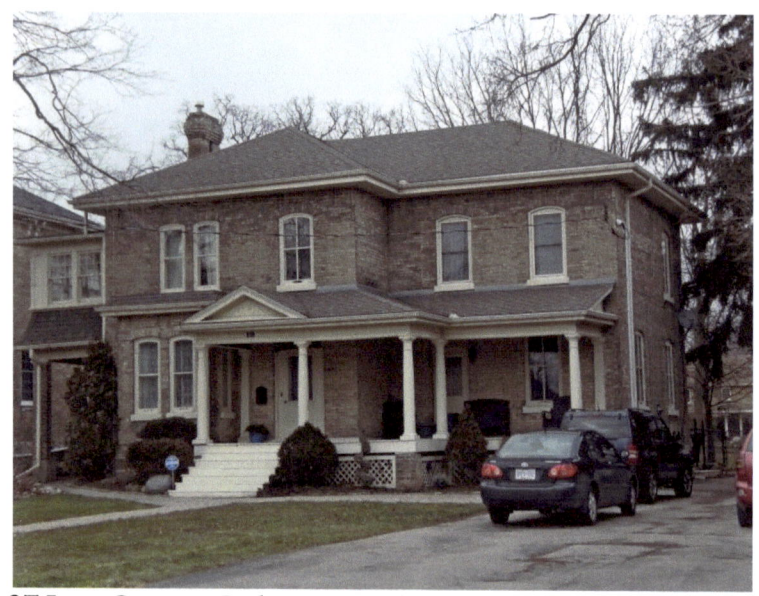

37 Jane Street – Italianate style – hipped roof, pediment

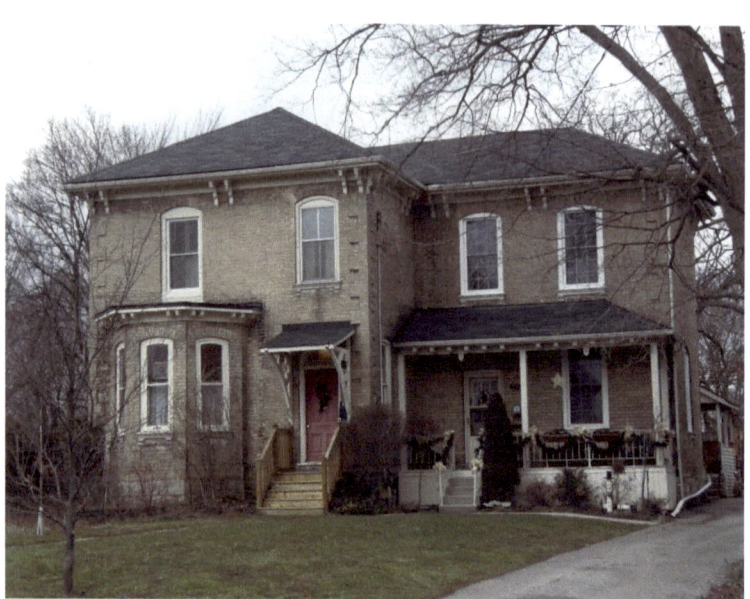

39 Jane Street – Italianate – paired cornice brackets, bay window, hipped roof

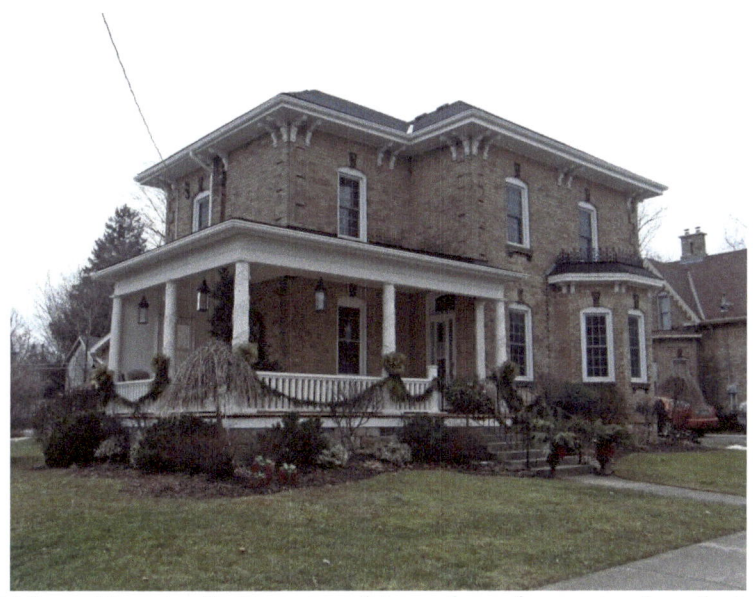

36 Jane Street – Italianate – hipped roof, cornice brackets, wraparound verandah, bay window

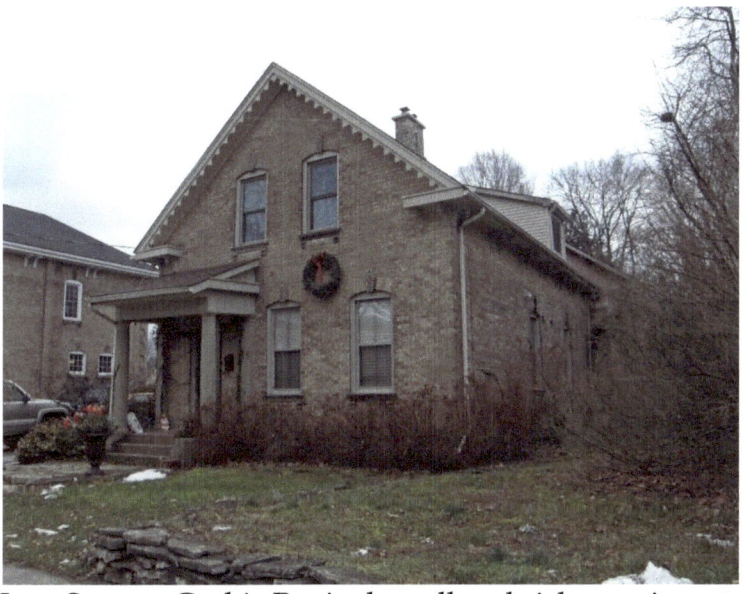

38 Jane Street – Gothic Revival – yellow brick, cornice return on gable, verge board trim

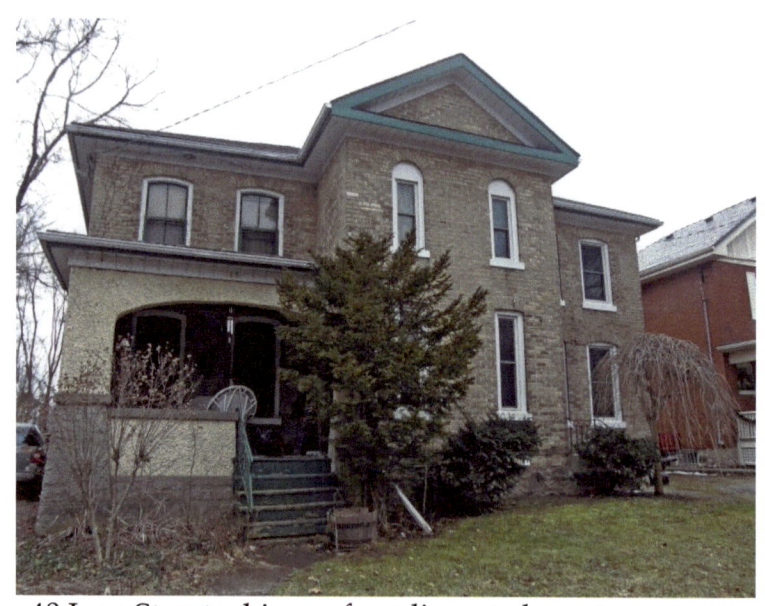

40 Jane Street – hip roof, pediment above two-storey frontispiece

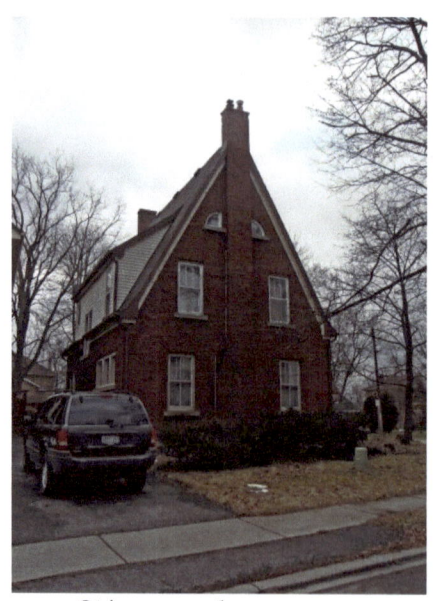

Jane Street – 2½ storey house, very steep gable

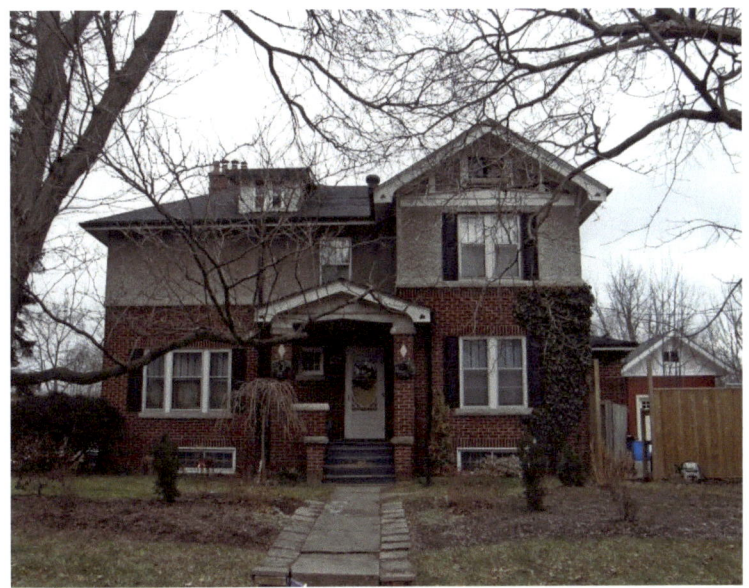

49 Jane Street – Italianate/Gothic mixture

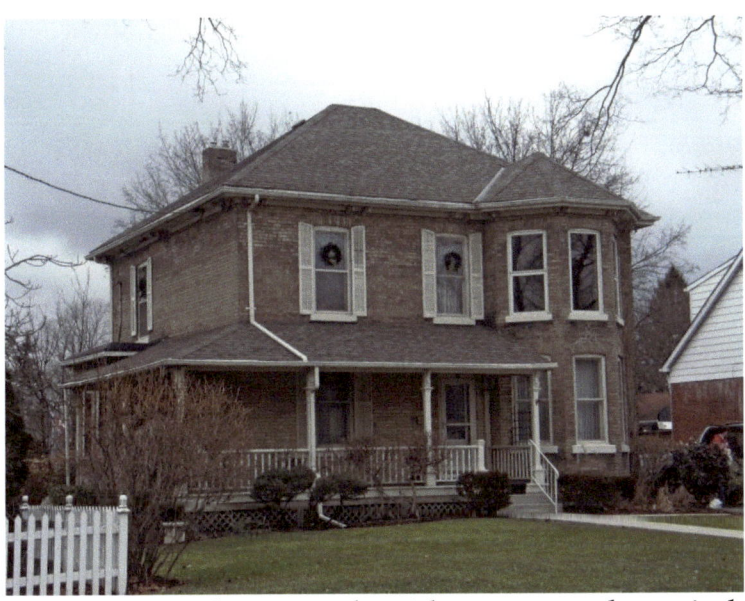

13 Jane Street – Italianate style with two-storey bay window, paired cornice brackets, yellow brick, hipped roof

Architectural Terms

Belvedere: (from the Italian "beautiful view") an architectural feature on a roof, in a garden or on a terrace that gives a beautiful view. Example: 165 Grand River Street North, Page 12	
Brackets: a decorative or weight-bearing structural element which forms a right angle with one side against a wall and the other under a projecting surface such as an eave or roof. Example: 36 Jane Street, Page 59	
Cobblestone architecture: Refers to the use of cobblestones embedded in mortar as a method for erecting walls on houses and commercial buildings. Example: 165 Grand River Street North, Page 12	
Cornice Return: decorative element on the end of a gable. Example: 28 Charlotte Street, Page 31	
Cupola: a small, dome-like structure on top of a building often used to provide a lookout or to admit light and air. Example: 184 Grand River Street North, Page 19	
Dichromatic brickwork: the use of two colours of brick, tile or slate to decorate a façade. Example: 184 Grand River Street North, Page 19	

Dormer: (French for "sleep") a gable end window that pierces through the plane of a sloping roof surface to create usable space in the top floor or attic of a building by adding headroom. Example: 26 Broadway Street East, Page 8	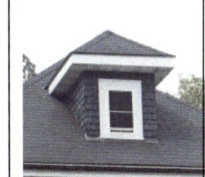
Frontispiece: a portion of the façade of a building, usually a centred doorway that is slightly raised from the rest of the building, usually with extensive ornamentation. Frontispieces are usually Classical in design with white columned porches. Example: 59-61 Banfield Street, Page 40	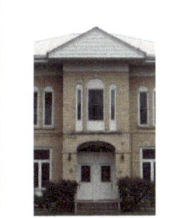
Gable: the triangular portion of a wall between the edges of a sloping roof. Example: 38 Banfield Street, Page 47	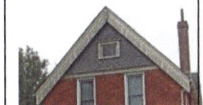
Hipped Roof: a roof where all sides slope downwards to the walls with no gables. Example: 11 Banfield Street, Page 52	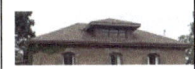
Iron Cresting: A decorative ornament along the top of a roof. Iron cresting was popular in the Baroque era and also in Italianate, Victorian, Second Empire and Queen Anne styles of architecture. Example: 184 Grand River Street North, Page 19	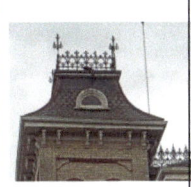

Keystones and Voussoirs: a voussoir is a wedge-shaped element used in building an arch. A keystone is the central stone that locks all the stones into position, allowing the arch to bear weight. A keystone is often enlarged and embellished. Example: 12 William Street, Page 29	
Palladian Window: a large window that is divided into three sections with the centre section larger than the two side sections and usually arched. Example: 18 Banfield Street, Page 50	
Pediment: a triangular section above the horizontal structure (entablature), typically supported by columns. The inside of the triangle is called the tympanum. Example: 38 Banfield Street, Page 47	
Quoin: masonry blocks at the corner of a wall, often a decorative feature, usually larger or of a different colour than the rest of the wall. Example: 55 Banfield Street, Page 42	
Rose Window: a circular window with ornamental tracery radiating from the centre. Example: 164 Grand River Street North, Page 13	

Sidelight: a vertical window that flanks a door, and is often used to emphasize the importance of a primary entrance. **Transom Window:** the light above the doorway, also called a fanlight. Example: 19 Broadway Street East, Page 6	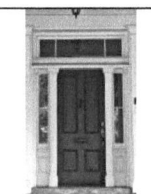
Tower: A circular, square, or octagonal vertical structure higher than the surrounding structure that is usually part of an existing building and is created either for extra defense or for a specific purpose such as a clock or a bell tower. Example: 185 Grand River Street North, Page 16	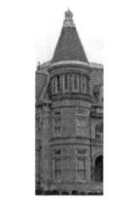
Turret: a small tower that projects from the wall of a building. Example: 18 Banfield Street, Page 50	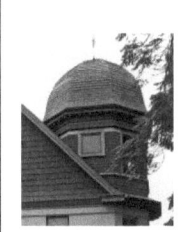
Verge boards: also called bargeboards – hang from the projecting end of a roof and are often elaborately carved and ornamented. **Finial:** ornament added to the top of a gable, pinnacle, canopy or spire – a Gothic element. Example: 104 West River Street, Page 37	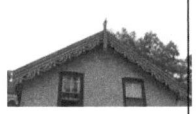

Building Styles

Edwardian, 1900-1930 – This style bridges the ornate and elaborate styles of the Victorian era and the simplified styles of the 20th century. Balanced facades, simple roof lines, dormer windows, large front porches, and smooth brick surfaces are its characteristics. Example: 18 Banfield Street, Page 50	
Georgian, before 1860 – This style began with the British King Georges in the 18th century. These buildings have balanced facades around a central door, medium-pitched gable roofs, and small paned windows. Example: 59-61 Banfield Street, Page 40	
Gothic Revival, 1830-1890 – These decorative buildings have sharply-pitched gables with highly detailed verge boards, pointed-arch window openings, and dichromatic brickwork. It is a common style in Ontario. Example: 38 Jane Street, Page 59	
Greek Revival – have gabled or hipped roofs with low pitches. The cornice of the main roof usually has a wide band which represents the entablature of classical Greek architecture consisting of the frieze and the architrave. Greek or Roman columns usually support the porch. The front door is surrounded by sidelights and a rectangular transom and is usually dressed with pilasters, pediments and/or columns. Example: 165 Grand River Street North, Page 12	

Italianate, 1850-1900 – It has wide-bracketed eaves, belvederes, wrap-around verandahs. Example: 184 Grand River Street North, Page 19	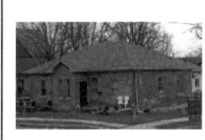
Regency Cottage, 1830-1860 – This style originated in England in 1815 and spread to Ontario later in the 19th century as British officers retired to Canada. It is a modest one-storey house with a low-pitched hip roof and has a symmetrical front façade. Example: 13 Broadway Street East, Page 7	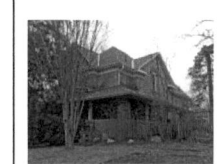
Queen Anne, 1885-1900 – This style is distinguished by an irregular outline featuring a combination of an offset tower, broad gables, projecting two-storey bays, verandahs, multi-sloped roofs, and tall, decorative chimneys. A mixture of brick and wood is common. Windows often have one large single-paned bottom sash and small panes in the upper sash. Example: Banfield Street, Page 45	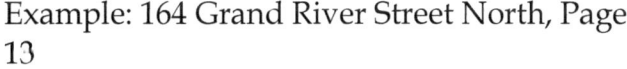
Romanesque Revival, 1880-1910 – This style hearkens back to medieval architecture of the 11th and 12th centuries with a heavy appearance, blocky towers and rounded arches. Example: 164 Grand River Street North, Page 13	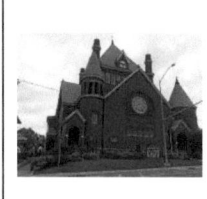

www.ingramcontent.com/pod-product-compliance
Lightning Source LLC
Chambersburg PA
CBHW040234220526
45473CB00001B/237